When will Jesus Christ return? Although the Bible warns us against setting dates for Christ's Second Coming, a number of Bible teachers continue to do so. As the dates have passed and Christ has *not* come, the evangelical church in America has had to battle ridicule of others and confusion within its own ranks. Disillusioned, some have even turned away from the faith.

Investigative reporter William Alnor probes the situation in this insightful and revealing book. Alnor cites cases, exposing the damage caused by nonbibical teaching. Yet he writes not to tear down the church, but to edify believers by exhorting us to obey Christ's command to reap the harvest before He returns.

When so many false teachers abound, how can you know whom to believe? This timely book will guide you in identifying *Soothsayers of the Second Advent*.

"Now brothers, about times and dates we do not need to write you, for you know very well that the day of the Lord will come like a thief in the night."

1 Thessalonians 5:1-2 (NIV)

When will Jesus Christ return? Although the Bible warns us against setting dates for Christ's Second Coming, a number of Bible teachers continue to do so. As the dates have passed and Christ has not come, the evangelical church in America has had to battle ridicule of others and confusion within its own ranks. Disillusioned, some have even turned away from the faith.

Investigative reporter William Alnor probes the situation in this insightful and revealing book. Alnor cites cases, exposing the damage caused by nonbiblical teaching, yet he writes not to tear down the church, but to edify believers by exhorting them to obey Christ's command to reap the harvest before He returns.

When so many false teachers abound, how can you know whom to believe? This timely book will guide you in identifying *Soothsayers of the Second Advent.*

"Now brothers, about times and dates we do not need to write you, for you know very well that the day of the Lord will come like a thief in the night."

1 Thessalonians 5:1-2 (NIV)

SOOTHSAYERS OF THE SECOND ADVENT

SOOTHSAYERS OF THE SECOND ADVENT

WILLIAM M. ALNOR

Power Books
Fleming H. Revell Company
Old Tappan, New Jersey

Library of Congress Cataloging-in-Publication Data

Alnor, William M.
Soothsayers of the Second Advent / William M. Alnor.
p. cm.
ISBN 0-8007-5324-0
1. Second Advent. 2. Prophecies—Controversial literature.
I. Title.
BT886.A46 1989 89-37133
236'.9—dc20 CIP

Published by the Fleming H. Revell Company
Old Tappan, New Jersey 07675
Printed in the United States of America

This book is lovingly dedicated to the memory of Dr. Walter R. Martin, who went home to be with the Lord on June 26, 1989. He inspired my wife and me to ". . . contend earnestly for the faith that was once for all entrusted to the saints" (Jude 3).

Contents

Part IV: Crediting the Occult and Other Questionable Practices

Part V: A Look Into the Future

Foreword

A few years ago while on a media lecture circuit, one of the best-known harbingers of the Second Advent told skeptical reporters at the Los Angeles Press Club how to recognize the Christ of All Religions.

"Lord Maitreya, the Christ" was living in a Pakistani section of London, waiting to be discovered by journalists, soberly declared Benjamin Creme, a white-haired British esotericist and author. When the Christ would soon reveal his true identity in the summer of 1982, Creme promised, "All the confusion and misunderstanding surrounding the Second Coming will be laid to rest."

The self-proclaimed way shower and follower of New Thought philosophy was aware that the Bible warns against false prophets and predicts that false Christs will arise before the true Messiah returns. "I meet them all the time," Creme told a reporter. "I have a file at home of what we call the 'false Christs.' I get all these letters. . . . There are dozens of them. Dozens."

Indeed. Through the years, I, too, have received dozens of letters —as well as callers—who claim to be the Messiah or his advance man.

In early 1976, a bearded young man made repeated trips to the *Los Angeles Times'* lobby, seeking to be interviewed. After several polite refusals by this religion writer, Messiah Ron grew more insistent. One morning he again showed up in the lobby and by telephone told me he was delivering an important hand-printed document that "must be published at once."

An alert copy messenger was dispatched to the lobby. "See if you can discourage this guy from coming back," I told her.

"This may come as quite a surprise to you," Messiah Ron began, handing the copy messenger a scroll. "I am the Messiah."

"Well," the young lady replied with aplomb, "this may come as quite a surprise to *you*, but you're the third messiah we've had here today!"

He has not returned.

Ron's message, which said it had "no human author," was to be published by all wire services and carried on all television networks on a specified date. The front-page headline for the *Times* was also dictated: "A Personal Message—The Lord Warns the World!"

As we fast approach the end of the second millennium, my guess is the tribe of soothsayers and self-appointed messiahs—and their publications—will increase manyfold. The year 2000 shines with an ominous, apocalyptic aura. But even in less auspicious times, humans seem to yearn for an eternal hero who will restore meaning to a disheveled world either by ushering in a Golden Age or by righteously presiding over history's final debacle.

William M. Alnor, in *Soothsayers of the Second Advent*, takes an in-depth look at the prophecy mongers, the rationale for their arguments, their motivations, and the uncritical acceptance accorded them by millions of Christian believers. In a journalistic fashion, Alnor shows how more than a few modern-day messengers twist Scripture—sometimes by innocent mistake, sometimes in egotistical zeal and self-delusion, and sometimes from a greedy desire to exploit people's fears and insatiable curiosity. Unscrupulous soothsayers rake in lucre from those who seek definite end-times timetables, down to the exact day and the hour of Jesus' return, Alnor relates.

Soothsayers of the Second Advent is needed. End-times watchers are herein warned to sidestep pitfalls that have entrapped many date setters, even as they appeal to the Scriptures that clearly forbid the very prognosticating that they do. Alnor points out the major players in the prophecy game. He elucidates how many of them, perhaps unwittingly, have mixed occult practices such as numerology, pyramidology, fortune-telling, and astrology with scriptural teachings and Christian eschatology, concocting a potent but deadly witch's brew.

But in his skillful debunking and exposing, Alnor doesn't ridicule the Bible's clear teaching that Jesus Christ will return. Nor does he dispatch the responsible prophecy scholars to the place reserved for the false prophets.

"Despite all the date setting, prediction, and speculation, nothing can change the fact that Jesus *will* come," Alnor writes near the end of this book. "He promises it in His Word; and just as He came the first time, fulfilling a host of prophecies, He will come again, fulfilling many more."

When that happens, we won't need Ben Creme or Messiah Ron to tell us it's for real.

Russell Chandler is a religion writer for the *Los Angeles Times* newspaper and author of the book *Understanding the New Age.*

Acknowledgments

I am very grateful to many people who were instrumental in helping put this book together. Frank Calamita, of Philadelphia, and Jay Trimble, of the Christian Information Bureau, in California, provided much documentation on the Southwest Radio Church. Rich Poll, of the Christian Research Institute, inspired us with good insights on contemporary Bible-prophecy teachers as he helped my wife and me wade through boxes of prophecy books and files at the institute's offices in Irvine, California. Poll also went over the manuscript and provided needed constructive criticism. My dad, Rev. Warren Alnor, Sr., of Niobrara, Nebraska, also went over the manuscript. I am also grateful to David Lewis of Springfield, Missouri, for his help.

Not every prophecy teacher discussed in this book cooperated with my efforts to examine their teachings. Thanks go to: Chuck Smith, Doug Clark, Salem Kirban, James McKeever, Charles Taylor, Hart Armstong, David Webber, and Noah Hutchings.

Last, but certainly not least, were the help and tremendous time my wife, Jacqueline, put toward the book. Actually, her name should also be on it with mine. The original concept of looking at modern-day prophecy errors to "rescue" true biblical prophecy was hers alone. She also contributed greatly in the research process. In fact, years before we even met, she had been collecting files on contemporary prophecy teachers. She also helped edit the manuscript and even helped write portions of it, including the conclusion. I thank God for teaming me up with this remarkable woman!

Introduction

We live in a world filled with " 'wars and rumors of wars. . . . Nation will rise against nation, and kingdom against kingdom. There will be famines and earthquakes in various places.' " Jesus' words in Matthew 24:6, 7 seem to describe today's newspaper. It is not surprising then that many Christians feel the countdown to Armageddon has already begun.

As life seems increasingly precarious on this planet Christians' eyes turn upward, looking for the return of Christ. Many even go so far as trying to fix dates and times to the events outlined in the books of Daniel and Revelation, in which the end of the world is prophesied. These soothsayers cannot resist the temptation to suit imaginary "horrifying" tales of the twentieth century into the pattern of Scripture.

Take, for example, the Antichrist. Ever since the Lord warned, "Little children, it is the last time: and as ye have heard that antichrist shall come . . ." (1 John 2:18 KJV), people have tried to put a name to the man who would so fully embody the spirit that opposes Christ.

Scores of modern-day prognosticators are more than willing to tell you his name. They do not seem to care whom they slander or whose reputation they drag through the mud. Some Christian ministries dedicate themselves to discerning the signs of the times for the church.

Their dedication may be admirable; their accuracy, however, is abysmal. They have made repeated grave errors in facts and judgment. I call them soothsayers of the Second Advent, and I call them that because they have attempted to use the Bible as a fortune-telling device to predict tomorrow's headlines.

Sometimes, in their zeal to warn people about the imminent return of Jesus Christ, they have brought discredit to God's Word through their inaccurate pronouncements. That's why this book was written—to separate prophetic fact from fantasy and to expose Second Coming fallacy in the very era when Jesus may indeed return to planet earth.

Without being too hard on our brethren—and undoubtedly most of the teachers mentioned in this book are brothers and sisters in Jesus Christ—I believe the day of reckoning is long overdue. Through shoddy research, sensationalism, reliance on unbiblical sources, ignorance, fear mongering, exclusive and dubious "revelations" and "visions," deliberate dishonesty, and misinterpretation of Scripture, they may have unwittingly helped set the scene for the final days of man.

Some have turned their speculations regarding the Second Coming of Christ into massive businesses and have profited handsomely from their wild guesses. Others, while claiming to be orthodox Christians, have relied on the occult to discern the signs of the times.

This book is a call for all teachers of Bible prophecy to match their own teachings with God's Word and His call for righteous judgment (John 7:24) and sober reasoning (1 Peter 4:7). These teachers who are heard over hundreds of radio stations and TV networks daily throughout the world think they are serving the Lord. Instead they are doing great damage to the cause of Christ. Rather than bringing men and women to the cross, they literally help fulfill a specific prophecy from the Apostle Peter:

> First of all, you must understand that in the last days scoffers will come, scoffing and following their own evil desires. They will say, "Where is this 'coming' he promised? Ever since our fathers died, everything goes on as it has since the beginning of creation."
>
> 2 Peter 3:3, 4

Indeed, many non-Christians are still scoffing because of a little booklet by Edgar C. Whisenant, called *88 Reasons Why the Rapture Will Be in 1988*, which was distributed to almost every pastor in America. The book, of which 3.2 million copies were printed,[1] sparked reports by the secular media that Christians were putting pets to sleep, selling all their goods, and going to hilltops to wait for the rapture. According to the book, the rapture was to take place September 11, 12, or 13, 1988. When it didn't happen, Whisenant did admit he was wrong—but only by a year—the rapture would happen in 1989.[2]

Besides causing non-Christians to scoff at the Second Coming, Whisenant and other soothsayers have done damage to immature believers. These prophecy teachers—and we're going to be dealing mostly with contemporary ones who have been influential within the past twenty years—have caused many to reject the doctrine of the imminent return of Christ, which is clearly taught in the Bible (Matthew 24:42–51). New Christians especially have been seriously wounded by the numerous false predictions.

It is baffling to see the same mistakes repeated over and over again in subsequent writings and messages, even after the harmful results of previous mistakes have been seen. Commented Charles R. Taylor, one of the most popular of the recent teachers, in his 1980 book, *Those Who Remain:*

> As time seemed to draw so near for the return of Christ, I wrote *Get all Excited—Jesus Is Coming Soon*. The evidence I presented caused such excitement among Christians that thousands of souls were led to a saving

> knowledge of Christ. . . . Because the book pointed strongly to the potential for our Lord's return in 1975 . . . some people lost their zeal by the end of the year. An attitude of lethargy and lukewarmness seemed to set in.[3]

Yet today Taylor still writes books, appears on television, and publishes newsletters hinting at revised dates for the return of Christ, the start of World War III, and the identity of the Antichrist, without apologizing to his supporters each time he has been wrong.

But some prophecy teachers have admitted their date-setting errors and freely talk about their mistakes today. These teachers—and we'll talk to some of them later—have learned something from their ill-fated predictions and have some insight about how Christians can avoid reading too much into today's newspaper headlines.

SOOTHSAYERS OF THE SECOND ADVENT

Part I
Prophetic Games Real Christians Play

Teachers who claim to have an inside track on the end times seem to specialize in three areas:

Antichrist naming
Rapture dating
Tribulation speculating

In order to understand them, we'll take a look at what the "experts" have said on these topics, what authority they have claimed as the basis for their words, and what the Bible says about their predictions.

Why do well-meaning Christians get derailed on the end-times train? Can we be specific regarding any details concerning Christ's return? How can we read and listen to the teachings of those who talk of the end times without boarding a train headed for disillusionment?

1
Pinning the Tail on the Antichrist

The place: Strasbourg, France.
The date: October, 1988.
The speaker: Pope John Paul II.

It was the key speech of the pope's four-day trip to France. Leaders from all across the continent had convened in Strasbourg for the European Parliament, and the pope had come to lend his support to the concept of a United States of Europe.

"A common political structure . . . far from endangering the identity of the people of the community, will be better suited to guarantee more fairly the rights . . . of all regions," said the pontiff.

Suddenly the Reverend Ian Paisley, a militant Protestant leader from Northern Ireland, jumped up and shouted, "I renounce you! I renounce you as the Antichrist!"

Paisley was instantly grabbed by ushers, and an orange banner was torn from his hands. The banner read: *Pope John Paul II, Antichrist.*

Ian Paisley isn't the first to dub someone with such a reprehensible label; since Christ foretold His return, people have enthusiastically played this game.

What Is an Antichrist?

Of all the men who wrote the Bible, only John uses the term *antichrist,* and he uses it only four times (1 John 2:18; 2:22; 4:3; 2 John 7).

In one sense John recognized antichrists in the first-century world—many of them, in fact—but he also speaks of "the antichrist . . . coming" (1 John 2:18). Other passages in Scripture, although they do not use the word *antichrist,* seem to identify this person more specifically.

When you put together this composite picture, you see the description of one powerful, political being who will hold sway over the earth in the end times. The following passages are frequently mentioned in prophetic views of the Antichrist:

The little horn	Daniel 7:8; 8:9
The ruler who will come	Daniel 9:25–27
The king who exalts himself	Daniel 11:36–45
The man of lawlessness	2 Thessalonians 2:3
The beast out of the sea	Revelation 13:1, 11–18; 19:20

The Antichrist will rule deceitfully (Daniel 11:23); he will deny and oppose God (1 John 2:22; Daniel 11:36, 37). He will even seek to proclaim himself God (2 Thessalonians 2:4). It's not hard to see that he will be a truly despicable fellow.

Antichrist, Antichrist, Who's Got the Antichrist?

Despite the overwhelmingly negative meaning of calling someone the Antichrist, Christians throughout the ages have never failed to try to plaster this name on the innocent—and not-so-innocent—political and spiritual leaders who have not met their fancy. During World War II many people thought Adolf Hitler was the Antichrist and that Benito Mussolini could be the false prophet referred to in Revelation 13. In the earliest Christian centuries, believers commonly thought the current Roman emperor—Nero, Domitian, Decius, Valerian, Diocletian—was the Antichrist, because of the savage persecutions waged by each one against Christianity.

Today, however, we might see the Antichrist tail pinned on leaders such as Jimmy Carter, Ronald Reagan, Henry Kissinger, or the pope.

One of the most active players in the "Pin the Tail on the Antichrist" game is Southwest Radio Church, aired by radio networks across the United States and overseas. Through the years, they have presented a very imposing lineup of possible Antichrists. But just when you feel ready to pin the tail on one of their candidates, they convince you that it is someone else.

For instance, in the 1976 edition of *Countdown for Antichrist*, David Webber, former president of the Oklahoma City based radio program, listed Austrian President Kurt Waldheim, former West German Chancellor Willy Brandt, the late Pope Paul VI, Prince Bernhard of the Netherlands, and Henry Kissinger as prime candidates. However, after naming the candidates, with an extensive section on why each one could be the satanic messiah, Webber threw in a disclaimer:

> I do not say, or even imply, that any of the five men I have mentioned is the Antichrist. I point them out to show you how it is possible for any number of men in the world today to be the beast who was, who is, and who is to come. One thing is for certain, he will be a man that the masses of the nations least suspect. He will be a man who will be respected and honored as a man of peace.[1]

Henry Kissinger?

Yes, Henry Kissinger.

In fact, in the 1984 edition of the same book, David Webber and Noah Hutchings cited the former United States secretary of state because of his phenomenal string of successes in shuttle diplomacy and alleged that Kissinger had many similarities that "match those of the coming world ruler." Someone even worked out a numbering system from Dr. Kissinger's name that adds up to 666.[2]

In the 1984 edition of the book, the names of Waldheim, Brandt, the late Pope Paul, and Prince Bernhard were dropped from the "suspect" list. No doubt it had something to do with the fact that Brandt's political star had waned, Waldheim was fighting allegations that he had been a Nazi death-camp guard, and Pope Paul VI had passed away in 1978. Probably the next edition will see Henry Kissinger's name deleted from the list as his political fortunes diminish.

The Antichrist prospect to watch, according to the Southwest Radio Church's June, 1987, the *Gospel Truth* newsletter is Karl Von Hapsburg, heir to the Hapsburg Austrian throne. David Webber says that Karl's father, Otto, is now "too old" to be the Antichrist. But since he proposed "a unified Europe with its old religious roots which, of course, meant a complete return to the Vatican . . . [his] 26-year-old son, Karl Von Hapsburg, who is becoming active in Common Market politics . . . bears watching in the future."[3]

Another candidate on the Southwest list is Libyan leader Moammar Qadhafi. According to Southwest's July, 1981, the *Gospel Truth*, "Qadhafi's messianic credentials qualify him in many respects as a candidate for Antichrist."

With Pope Paul VI stricken from the slate, Pope John Paul II has taken his place. Southwest Radio Church's Noah Hutchings, agreeing with Ian Paisley, clearly implied that John Paul II has the credentials in an article called "The Vatican Connection," in the April, 1984, issue of the *Gospel Truth*. Using Revelation 13:2–8, which describes the Antichrist's ascent to power after he is inflicted with a seemingly fatal wound, Hutchings paralleled that with the assassination attempt on the pope's life in the early 1980s:

> In Pope John Paul II we see a man who is rising in international stature, a man who will be increasingly called upon to bring peace to a troubled world. His recovery from a deadly wound directed world atten-

> tion and admiration to his personage, and he, like those before him, would seemingly like to establish his authority over the Holy Hill of Zion.
>
> It is not our intention to draw any prophetic conclusions.
>
> We have attempted only to report these events and leave eschatological parallels to the discernment of the individual reader.[4]

Soviet leader Mikhail Gorbachev has also been getting quite a few tails pinned on him. In 1989 Southwest Radio Church was offering Robert W. Faid's book *Gorbachev! Has the Real Antichrist Come?* for a "love gift" of six dollars. It may seem strange to send a love gift to determine who the Antichrist is, but that's the way it is when you play "Pin the Tail on the Antichrist."

Of course, the Southwest Radio Church hasn't been the only player in the game.

- In her self-published book, *A Planned Deception,* lawyer Constance Cumbey draws upon New Age author Peter LeMesurier to explore the possible appearance of a new "messiah" in Israel in 1986.[5]

  But she became suspicious of Christian broadcaster Pat Robertson because of his long-time commitment to broadcasting in the Middle East and because of his presidential aspirations. So she began honing in on him as a candidate for the Antichrist, despite Robertson's clear Christian testimony. In her speaking engagements across the United States, Cumbey, author of the controversial book exposing the New Age movement, *Hidden Dangers of the Rainbow,* repeatedly announced her fears and stated that Robertson had hypnotic powers over people and that he hypnotized evangelist Jimmy Swaggart into supporting his bid for the presidency.[6] When Robertson got wind of Cumbey's charges, he threatened to sue her.[7]
- For years, on his television program, "Today in Bible Prophecy," seen coast to coast on several cable networks, popular prophecy teacher Charles R. Taylor has been pushing King

Juan Carlos of Spain as his Antichrist nomination. In his 1980 edition of *Those Who Remain,* Taylor stated that could be the year Carlos would be revealed as the Antichrist. "Could it be King Juan Carlos I, and could the year be 1980?" he asked. "Time alone will tell, but existing evidence indicates that it is a distinct possibility."[8] Taylor said he first began eyeing Carlos as the Antichrist in 1974.[9]

- Prophecy teacher Mary Stewart Relfe had another candidate: Egypt's Anwar Sadat. Her first book, *When Your Money Fails,* became a best-seller, with more than 700,000 copies published in eleven printings.[10] The book established her as one of the more extreme prophecy teachers. In her 1982 sequel, *The New Money System,* she published her own list of Antichrist candidates: "Henry Kissinger, (King) Juan Carlos (of Spain), Pope John Paul II, and Anwar Sadat."[11]

  "After giving much time to studying the scriptural qualifications, characteristics, and prerequisites, my prudent assessment is that President Anwar Sadat of Egypt is either history's nearest prototype or the real Mr. '666'," she wrote.[12] Her assessment wasn't prudent enough. Sadat was assassinated in 1981, and his deadly wound was not healed.
- Additionally, prophecy teacher Doug Clark, whose popular show, "Shockwaves of Armageddon" (formerly called "Amazing Prophecies"), is televised coast-to-coast, announced in 1976 that President Jimmy Carter would be "the president who will meet Mr. 666 (the Antichrist) SOON!" A flier announcing Clark's new book that year, screamed, "THE DEATH OF THE UNITED STATES and THE BIRTH of ONE WORLD GOVERNMENT under President Carter."

Others have also focused on Jimmy Carter as having a key role in the revealing of the Antichrist to the world. Even as late as June, 1983, James McKeever, a prophecy teacher who heads Omega Ministries, reprinted in *End Times News Digest* an article that questioned what former President "Carter was really doing in Israel." According to the story, Carter was really in Israel to prepare for the unveiling of the Antichrist.

Others have had even more fantastic views of the Antichrist. In his book, *AD 1991—the Genesis of Holocaust,* Henry R. Hall cites a vision by astrologer-psychic Jeane Dixon and his own exclusive revelation to state:

> This Antichrist could be revealed in early 1992 as he could be (if Dixon's vision was accurate) exactly thirty years old on February 5th, 1992.
>
> One revelation that I had prior to my discovery of Mrs. Dixon's vision was that not only was the Antichrist already born but that, as of the date of my revelation (March 1984), he was at the age of 23.[13]

Hall *didn't* mention that Scripture *always* condemns the use of astrology and divination, both openly practiced by Mrs. Dixon.

At one point even the well-respected leader Pat Robertson engaged in some guessing about the age of the Antichrist. In a 1980 issue of his *Perspective* newsletter Robertson stated (in a quote critics used to lampoon him during his unsuccessful 1988 bid for the presidency), "And if the antichrist is yet to come, then we must conclude that there is a man alive today, approximately 27 years old, who is being groomed to be the Satanic messiah."[14]

The Mark of the Antichrist

Modern-day soothsayers also come up with some guesses regarding the mark of the Antichrist. In Webber's 1976 edition of *Countdown for Antichrist,* he stated that the peace symbol, a popular sign of the hip Woodstock generation, could be it. "We have no reason for believing that it will be anything but an emblem or insignia," he reasoned. "The mark of antichrist could be the modern peace symbol, or some form thereof. We know that by peace the antichrist will gain power over the nations, and we can think of no better anti-type of the cross than the broken cross."[15]

Likewise, the premise of Relfe's books is that the number

666—identified in Revelation 13 as the mark of the beast—is already here, and we're already using it! It's the supermarket bar codes, she claims![16] But Relfe has erred by not mentioning that the Bible clearly states that people will deliberately take the mark on their hands or foreheads in order to buy or sell and to show allegiance to the future dictator. Scripture *never* implies that people will be unaware that they are using it.

Is This True?

Scripture provides us with some clear commands concerning our outlook on the end times and the faith we should put in the words of those who seek to clarify prophetic Scriptures.

The Work God Has for Us. Forty days after the Resurrection, the disciples asked Jesus to reveal the secrets of His return. He responded by giving His last command before He returned to heaven. Because it *was* His last command, we need to give it our special attention. " 'It is not for you to know the times or dates the Father has set by his own authority,' " Jesus warned (Acts 1:7).

In other words, Jesus was saying, "Stop playing 'Pin the Tail on the Antichrist' and get down to the really important business." He described their real work with His next words: " 'But you will receive power when the Holy Spirit comes on you; and you will be my witnesses in Jerusalem, and in all Judea and Samaria, and to the ends of the earth' " (Acts 1:8). God's power gives believers the ability to do the work He has for them—telling others of Him. Gazing idly into the clouds is not what He planned for Christians.

When someone begins to reinterpret God's Word according to today's headlines, we need to keep in mind the advice Paul gave Timothy about some teachers in his area:

> . . . Command certain men not to teach false doctrines any longer nor to devote themselves to myths

> and endless genealogies. These promote controversies rather than God's work—which is by faith. The goal of this command is love, which comes from a pure heart and a good conscience and a sincere faith. Some have wandered away from these and turned to meaningless talk. They want to be teachers of the law, but they do not know what they are talking about or what they so confidently affirm.
>
> 1 Timothy 1:3–7

Do the predictions of some of today's prophecy teachers have the same effect as the first-century genealogies? Are we hearing meaningless talk? Do the end-time teachers really know what they are talking of?

There is a danger in meaningless talk. Paul added:

> Timothy, guard what has been entrusted to your care. Turn away from godless chatter and the opposing ideas of what is falsely called knowledge, which some have professed and in so doing have wandered from the faith. . . .
>
> 1 Timothy 6:20, 21

How do we know if what we hear about the end of the age *is* godless chatter? Should we ignore *all* we hear?

No, for the Bible has given us clear signposts, which are increasingly evident. We have no need to fabricate or sensationalize stories while man is clearly on a collision course with destiny.

Instead we need to consider the whole counsel of God, as shown in His Word. Like the Bereans, let us examine the Scriptures, to see if what we hear is true (Acts 17:11). As actual events take place—such as the return of the Jews to their homeland—we can exclaim as did the disciples, "Did he not tell us in advance?" (*see* John 2:22).

2
88 Reasons Wasn't Enough

The Trinity Broadcasting Network (TBN) altered their regular programming on September 11–13, 1988. Instead of airing their regular nightly "Praise the Lord" television talk show, founders Paul and Jan Crouch decided to run selected videotapes.

The subject matter was the same on all the prerecorded shows—the rapture. Specifically the messages instructed nonbelieving viewers what to do if their loved ones—believers in Christ—suddenly disappeared.

September 11–13, 1988, was the Jewish Feast of Trumpets or Rosh Hashanah. But to Christians curious about Bible prophecy it was also the target date on which Edgar C. Whisenant, a former NASA engineer, told the world that Christ would rapture the church into heaven, leaving the Christ-rejecting world behind to face God's wrath in the tribulation, referred to in the book of Revelation. His little book caused an incredible stir.

It was not his teaching that a rapture would take place that caused the furor. Scripture nowhere uses the word *rapture*, but it describes Christians as being caught up at the return of the Lord (1 Thessalonians 4:16, 17; 2 Thessalonians 2:1).

No, it was not his teaching about the fact of the rapture, but rather, according to the title of his little book, that he knew eighty-eight reasons why Jesus would return in 1988. Nearly every evangelical Christian in America was at least aware of Whisenant's predictions. For several days leading up to that date, the folks at Trinity (and in Christian circles everywhere) were talking about the rapture, Jan Crouch personally testifying that Whisenant's reasoning was impressive. "What if it really does happen?" some asked. Some laughed, many others dared not.

Whisenant wasn't the only one implying a 1988 rapture. Norvell L. Olive, of the World Bible Society, wrote in the foreword of Whisenant's booklet *On Borrowed Time* (that accompanied *88 Reasons*), that Brother Joseph Civelli of Pensacola, Florida, calculated the same dates as Whisenant for "the Rapture, Armegedden [sic] and the Second Advent."[1]

Up-and-coming prophecy teacher J. R. Church (whom Whisenant quotes in *88 Reasons*) in his *Hidden Prophecies in the Psalms* clearly implied a 1988 rapture.[2] Hart Armstrong, president of Christian Communications, of Wichita, Kansas, repeatedly did it throughout 1988, pinpointing the Feast of Trumpets, 1988, "or September 29, 30, 1989, as possible times for His coming," and issuing a "RAPTURE ALERT" in his publications.[3] Charles Taylor planned his 1988 tour of Israel to coincide with Whisenant's date, with the possibility of being raptured from the Holy Land as a sales incentive: ". . . only $1975 from Los Angeles or $1805 from New York (and return if necessary)," said his *Bible Prophecy News*.[4] In a later pitch for the tour, he stated: "We stay at the Intercontinental Hotel right on the Mount of Olives where you can get the beautiful view of the Eastern Gate and the Temple Mount. And if this is the year of our Lord's return, as we anticipate, you may even ascend to Glory from within a few feet of His ascension."[5]

Following the failure of Whisenant's prediction, in his

September–October, 1988, *Communicare* newsletter, Armstrong at first said that he has "No Apologies! No Excuses! No Explanations!" and "No Regrets!" for agreeing with Whisenant's dates. But in the next month's newsletter he confessed that he took things "too far" in suggesting a possible date. In the next newsletter—November, 1988—he wrote that he was "very concerned—not worried—by the fact that 'the bottom fell out' during September on our income that comes in by mail from our friends." He added that he received some critical letters from "preachers who felt it their duty to discipline me" for setting dates. Then he added: "I have confessed my error, and assured you I would never again suggest a date for Christ's coming." Since that time Armstrong has been true to his word about specific dates. But in his March, 1989, devotional letter he wrote that he is dedicating his personal life partly to the "task of sounding forth the 'Rapture Alert.' "

Of course, since the publication of Lindsey's *The Late Great Planet Earth*, 1988 had become a magical year to prophecy students. A major thesis in Lindsey's best-seller was that the Hebrew prophets spoke of a time when the earth would face God's judgment and wrath. Jesus said there would be one generation in which all future events would climax with His own Second Coming. Lindsey pointed out that a key event touching off God's prophetic clock would be the return of the Jews to the land of Israel, which became a historical fact in 1948. He concluded that since a biblical generation is forty years, all one has to do is add forty to 1948.

What Went Wrong?

The amazing thing about Whisenant's forecast is that so many people took it seriously. After Whisenant proved to be wrong, many disenchanted believers couldn't really say why. Analyzing his *88 Reasons* will provide us with a good study, since striking parallels exist between it and the teachings of almost all of today's soothsayers of the Second Advent.

Although Whisenant's booklet was short—fifty-eight pages long—he committed almost all the major contemporary prophecy errors: He relied on pyramidology, astrology, numerology, subjective revelation, mathematical calculations, and questionable sources to come up with his reasonings.

But perhaps the most serious error Whisenant has made is to name the date of Christ's Second Advent—something strictly forbidden by Jesus Himself (*see* Matthew 24:36). Whisenant countered this charge on radio commercials heard across America by saying that even though Jesus said we can't know the day and hour of His return, we can know the year, the month, and the week.

In his "88 Reasons What Went Wrong" article, which appeared in the Fall, 1988, *Christian Research Journal*, Dean C. Halverson, a former researcher for the Spiritual Counterfeits Project, dissects Whisenant's errors. The following assessment borrows from his evaluation.

Whisenant's first problem is that after he was proven wrong, he began to backpedal, setting even more dates for the rapture. He set an October 3 date, and when that failed, he declared: "It is going to be in a few weeks anyway."[6] When that date passed, instead of repenting for his errors, Whisenant claimed his calculations were "one year off" and that Christ would return during Rosh Hashanah (September 30), 1989,[7] or at the end of the Feast of Tabernacles (October 14–20).[8]

To further "prove" we can know the time of the Lord's return, Whisenant twists Matthew 24:36, where Jesus says, regarding the time of the end of the age, "No one knows about that day or hour. . . ." Whisenant says that while we cannot know it "instinctively," with "*some effort*" we can "*perceive and understand it*." But according to Halverson, Whisenant has turned "the meaning of the verse on its head. Whereas Jesus is clearly saying that we cannot predict the time of His second coming, Whisenant has Him instead saying that with enough research we can predict the time, down to the very week."[9]

Whisenant does similar manipulations with Jesus' words in Acts 1:7, where the disciples are told: "It is not for you to know the times or dates [*seasons,* in some translations]. . . ."

Whisenant argues that while we will not know the "day and hour" of Christ's return, we *will* know the times and seasons—even down to the exact week. This is again the opposite of what Jesus said. In Matthew we are told that we will not know the day or the hour; in Acts we are told we will not know even the month or year of His return.

In two other errors, Whisenant concludes we can know the week of Christ's coming by His use of the flood of Noah's day and Jesus' parable of the ten virgins. Concerning the flood, which Jesus referred to in Matthew 24:37–41, Whisenant says that the flood wasn't a surprise appearance either; God certainly told Noah about it. Of the ten virgins (Matthew 25:1–13) Whisenant said they were alerted by the shout "the bridegroom cometh." Today he claims the book, *88 Reasons,* is the shout.[10]

But Halverson points out that Jesus specifically used the flood analogy, combined with the "thief in the night" parable (Matthew 24:42–44), to tell us that "you also must be ready, because the Son of Man will come at an hour when you do not expect him." And in the case of the ten virgins, the point of the parable clearly is that we are supposed to be ready for his coming *before* the shout.[11]

It is also troubling that Whisenant has such an exclusive view of his role in the Second Coming as to refer to his book as God's shout. In a February, 1989, *Charisma & Christian Life* magazine interview, Whisenant stated his ministry "is the final movement of God," while relying on subjective—and questionable—visions and revelations that God's final movement would come from his hometown in Arkansas in the last days. "By the way, God did say that His last movement would come out of Little Rock. I live in Little Rock. I believe this is it," he said. ". . . Corrie ten Boom saw it in a vision. And Kathryn Kuhlman said it would."[12]

Whisenant also relied on the testimony of astrologer-psychic Jeane Dixon for some of his reasons (64 and 65). Astrology and divination are condemned outright in the Scriptures, yet these are the methods Dixon employs to look into future events. In addition Whisenant relies on numerology, which is also linked with the occult. He delves into speculations about the Great Pyramid of Giza as signs of the end in reason 77. He relies on extensive mathematical calculations—not the clear Word of God that tells us to be ready always for His coming—for other reasons.

These are only some reasons for concern and surprise that so many believers took Whisenant seriously. The fact that Whisenant relied on an astrologer and unbiblical means to calculate the Second Coming should have been reason enough to dismiss him immediately without looking any further. As Halverson said so well in the *Christian Research Journal:* "The practice of speculating about the date of the Rapture is akin in spirit to that of the diviners and astrologers (Deut. 18:9–14; Is. 47:12–14). It is akin in that they all seek after a knowledge that is reserved for God alone."

Could it be that when Peter predicted that in the last days there will come scoffers saying, "Where is the promise of his coming" (*see* 2 Peter 3:3, 4), it would be fulfilled as a knee-jerk reaction to highly publicized soothsayers like Whisenant?

Already Whisenant had caused some chuckles to come from within the church. "Dear Editor," said a letter from an Iowa woman, published in the April, 1989, issue of *Charisma & Christian Life*. "I can't wait for Edgar Whisenant's new book: *89 Reasons Why the Rapture Will Be in 1989*. Know what his 89th reason will be? 'Because it wasn't in '88.' "

3
Tribulation Just Around the Corner . . . I Think

It might seem bad enough that one has to contend with the Antichrist namers and the rapture daters, but there are also the tribulation timers.

Despite all the Bible's warnings not to be concerned with such things, Christians have attempted to predict the date when the great suffering preceding the Second Coming will occur.

Of this time, Scripture says:

- There will be unequaled distress in the world as God pours out His wrath on humankind (Matthew 24:21; Revelation 16:1).
- Nations will rise up against one another, troubles will cover the earth, and fearful events will occur in the heavens (Luke 21:10, 11).
- False prophets will appear and claim to be the Christ. They will seek to deceive even those who know Him (Matthew 24:22–24; Revelation 16:13, 14).
- There will be a great battle at Armegeddon (Revelation 16:16).

- After that distress, the sun and moon will no longer give light; the heavenly bodies will be disrupted (Matthew 24:29).
- At that time, the Son of Man will appear in the skies "with power and great glory" (Matthew 24:30).

Tribulation Timers

Not satisfied with such descriptions, many teachers have tried to look into the future and predict events that fit the pattern set by God's Word. Something about the imminent return of the Lord seems to draw avid speculation!

Charting the Future

Divine Revelations? In 1983 Mary Stewart Relfe wrote that she had been praying to "know the year" of the Lord's coming. That, she claims, resulted in dreams and "divine revelations." She saw World War III just ahead, resulting in the "partial destruction of the U.S. due to nuclear attack." It was "one of the most tremendous 'divine revelations' I have ever received from the Lord."[1]

She released a detailed chart claiming World War III would happen in 1989. In 1990, the "Great Tribulation Begins," and Jesus Christ will come back in 1997, "just after Armageddon." She also predicts a "total destruction of the U.S. 3–4 years before Armageddon as revealed to me in Scripture."

Her source for these claims? "The overall time element is based upon divine revelation. . . . Since I was praying at that time to 'know the year,' I believe this chart is accurate to within one year. Dates of lesser details are prudent assessments."[2]

What's in a Year? Relfe is not alone in her penchant for dating the tribulation. Edgar Whisenant attempted to make a most exacting tribulation chart. But of course his failed 1988 rapture has disrupted his timetable, so now he asserts he was one year off in his calculations and has pushed it all back to 1989.

If his chart was pushed back exactly one year, the two prophetic witnesses of Revelation 11 were rescheduled to arrive on September 26, 1989, and the 144,000 Jews referred to in Revelation 7 have already begun preaching God's Word about Jesus.[3]

If we move up other dates on the chart back a year to agree with Whisenant's statements that he was off by one year, October 4, 1989, would signify the end of World War III, which would have lasted less than a day. Within another day, the Antichrist would have power over the Roman Empire's nations. On April 19, 1992, the Antichrist "dies at sunset and goes to hell." On December 23, 1996, the millennium begins at sunset.[4]

Henry Kreysler (Watchman in the Wilderness) of Desert Hot Springs, California, has also set some rash dates. In a five-tape prophecy collection he advertises in *Charisma & Christian Life* magazine, he includes a last-days chart. His chart, called a "proposed scenario for the End of this present evil age," has Russia invading Israel in 1988 and calls the 1986 Chernobyl nuclear accident in Russia a possible "trumpet" of the book of Revelation. He lists the rapture of the church and the abomination of desolation in 1991, with a 1995 Armageddon.

Purveyor of a Hidden Message. Reginald Dunlop, California author of several self-published books on the end times, prophesied: "Worldwide famine by 1986 . . . many will die as a result . . . the United States will feel hunger pains for the first time. . . ."[5] It would be so bad that "human body parts will be sold in stores."[6] The Antichrist would be revealed "around the year 1989 or 1990, perhaps sooner."[7] The rapture would be in 1991.

God verified this, Dunlop says, "through many prayers. . . . I am MORE than positive that this is THE YEAR that the Rapture will occur."[8]

How does he know what is hidden from others? Dunlop claims to be part of a "small circle of His specially initiated people" who can interpret prophecy.[9]

Charting Southwest Radio Church. It's hard to outdo the Southwest Radio Church in Bible-prophecy speculation. Does this ministry ever have charts! The problem is, they keep issuing new ones because previous charts have failed.

For example, David Webber and Noah Hutchings's book *Prophecy in Stone* contains a chart called "The Time of Christ's Coming," which includes these dates: "Jewish Temple Rebuilt? 1974–1978; beginning of the Tribulation, 1981–1985; end of the Tribulation, 1988–92."[10]

When most of those dates came and went, the book went out of print. In its place, Southwest Radio Church published *New Light on the Great Pyramid,* by the same authors, which included a revised date table. Oddly enough, the books are exact duplicates, except for the new date chart and a new chapter in the revised version about the alleged discovery of a pyramid on the planet Mars. The revised dates tentatively set the beginning of the tribulation for 1988, the abomination of desolation for 1992, and Christ's coming for 1996.[11]

Was their "new" book deceptive? Hutchings and Webber don't think so. Hutchings said that in the first book the date table was done by a local pastor, who "later changed his opinion or ideas or teachings about the Second Coming."

It "was so confusing that we just took it out because he had changed his viewpoints, so we . . . amended it," Hutchings said, claiming that in the date table in the new version he didn't engage in date setting, because beside every suggested date he placed a question mark. (Apparently the new dates, like the prior chart, are not "set in stone.")

Webber and Hutchings said the change was not due to their date-table failure. The original publisher went bankrupt, so they simply reissued the book under another title. "We were supposed to get royalties out of it, and we never received a penny. So we just changed the name of the book," added Hutchings, claiming the original book sold 250,000 copies.[12]

So what other dates have Webber and Hutchings suggested? Their book *Is This the Last Century?* foresaw a 1981–

1988 tribulation period.[13] Later, they expected the rapture of the church and the beginning of the tribulation "possibly in 1987 or 1988."[14] Other Southwest Radio Church literature hinted at a 1982 rapture, to coincide with the Jupiter Effect.

In a recent interview Webber said he has *never* set dates. Any timetables published by his ministry are only "suggested" timetables, and there's nothing wrong with that, he said. "I never said that the Lord had to come in 1981 and any timetables that we suggest that have to do with Israel are *suggested* timetables," Webber said. "I don't think we ever said dogmatically that this timetable is rigid and will come to pass.

"It's not all right to set projected dates. We've never done that; we may have suggested that perhaps '81 was a good time for the Lord to come. We hoped that maybe He would, but we didn't establish it or say, 'Hey, the Lord has to come on Rosh Hashanah, 1981 or '88.' "

Jesus *Will* Return About. . . . North Carolina prophecy teacher Colin Deal has also rearranged the timing of end-time events. In his 1979 book *Christ Returns by 1988: 101 Reasons Why*, Deal wrote, "Christ will return bodily to the earth or in the air for the church by 1988."[15] He also said that he thought the rapture would be in 1982 or 1983.[16] But two years later Deal's new book, *The Day and Hour Jesus Will Return*, placed Christ's return "at approximately 1989."[17] He also enclosed a chart with the book listing the "Start of Tribulation" in "1982(?)"[18]

But Deal, heard on the Southwest Radio Church's broadcast on March 17, 1989, changed his tune again. His new claim is that Christ's return is about "eleven years away" (not counting His coming for the church in the rapture, seven years prior to that—about four years from the broadcast).

A Mass of Speculations. Many others, caught up in last-days fever, have speculated on dates. Pat Robertson, for example, once suggested a 1982 tribulation, sparked by a Russian invasion of Israel.[19] Lester Sumrall, founder of

LeSEA Broadcasting, said in his book, *I Predict 2000 A.D.*: "I predict the absolute fullness of man's operation on planet Earth by the year 2000 A.D. Then Jesus Christ shall reign from Jerusalem for 1000 years."[20]

Whom Do You Believe?

With all the date setting and retracting that goes on, it's hard to keep score. One might even feel tempted to believe it's a big mistake and that Jesus really didn't plan to come again at all.

To keep our heads and hearts clear, we need to take a look at what the teachers are saying and what the Bible says about their predictions.

Have They Really Heard From God?

Has Mary Stewart Relfe really heard directly from God about the tribulation times? Does Reginald Dunlop have some special knowledge the rest of us have missed?

No!

Look at Relfe's view of future events, according to her chart. For 1983 it's, "Begin water storage. Accumulate canning jars/lids, and start buying food for a month ahead." In 1984 her advice was to try to locate a rural survivalist retreat. For 1985 she prophesied: "Credit cards emerge into debit cards. Inflation begins to accelerate with liberal Democrat in the White House. Move out of the Northeast (WW III), and the Southwest (Mexico problems). The more remote the better. Retreat must have good water supply." For 1988 she claims God showed her the "great exodus to rural America begins en masse, and increasingly to other nations. Big Brother closes in. Only 'State' Church approved."[21]

The liberal Democrat she prophesied America would elect to the presidency did not make it to the White House. Instead one of the most popular presidents in history held the office—conservative Republican Ronald Reagan. Many of her other prophesies have also failed.

Scripture warns: "Test everything. Hold on to the good" (1 Thessalonians 5:21) and ". . . do not believe every spirit, but test the spirits to see whether they are from God, because many false prophets have gone out into the world" (1 John 4:1). We *can* test the prophecies we hear—in fact, we *have* to!

How do we know a prophetic utterance is from God? According to Deuteronomy 18:21, 22, we are to judge prophets on the basis of their accuracy. In Old Testament times, prophetic utterances that were any less than 100 percent correct were punished by death by stoning (Deuteronomy 13:1–11). Though I am not suggesting that you throw rocks at anyone, you can use this as a key to discernment.

Reginald Dunlop fares no better than Relfe, though he claims a special initiation. How could his words come from the God of the Bible, when they do not perfectly hold to His Word?

Nor can other teachers play on words by saying they have "suggested" dates. Many of those who draft tribulation charts that date coming events use methods such as "divine revelation," mystical interpretations of Scripture, and mathematical calculations to support their claims. But they have ignored this admonition of the Apostle Paul: "Now brothers, about times and dates we do not need to write you, for you know very well that the day of the Lord will come like a thief in the night. While people are saying, 'Peace and safety,' destruction will come on them suddenly . . ." (1 Thessalonians 5:1–3).

God has not revealed all to us, and who can know His infinite mind well enough to speculate on the things He has not revealed? When we go beyond what is written in Scripture of the end times, we go beyond His will—out into our own territory of invention. Instead of practicing fanciful arts, 2 Timothy 2:15 admonishes us to present ourselves to God as approved workmen who do not need to be ashamed and who correctly handle the word of truth.

Just as Paul went on to warn against "godless chatter"

and cite Hymenaeus and Philetus "who have wandered away from the truth. They say that the resurrection has already taken place, and they destroy the faith of some" (2 Timothy 2:16–18), we need to beware of teachers in our day who make claims about end-times dating. Like those who believed Hymenaeus and Philetus, the faith of today's Christians can be shaken.

If we honestly read Scripture, we will see that we can't make even general statements, speculations, or predictions about the date of *any* end-time event. How can we avoid the evidence of Matthew 24:26; Mark 13:32; 1 Thessalonians 5:1–3; and Acts 1:7? All agree in their message: No one will know the times the Father has set.

The Lesson in Date Setting

We could all learn from Chuck Smith of Calvary Chapel, Costa Mesa, California. Smith could have once been considered a date setter. In his 1978 book, *Future Survival,* he wrote: "From my understanding of biblical prophecies, I'm convinced that the Lord is coming for His Church before the end of 1981. I could be wrong, but it's a deep conviction in my heart, and all my plans are predicated upon that belief."[22]

Today Smith is under the conviction that setting any kind of date or timetables for things that are in God's hands is wrong. He says we can believe in the "imminency of the return of Christ without setting dates" because "no one knows the day or the hour. However, Paul said of the times and the seasons we are not ignorant that that day should catch us unaware."

> Date setting is wrong, and I was guilty of coming close to that. I did believe that Hal Lindsey could have been on the track when he talked about the forty-year generation, the fig tree budding being the rebirth of Israel, and I was convinced in my own heart. I never did teach it as scriptural dogma, but I had a personal

> conviction that Christ was coming before 1982. . . . I've learned that we can not put any parameters on the return—or on the rapture of the church—there are no parameters—it can happen at any time, hopefully within our lifetime but maybe not.[23]

4
What Profit Is Prophecy?

Because there have been so many abuses, over the centuries, in discerning the signs of the times, many Bible teachers and ministers today practically ignore Bible prophecy.

Some evangelicals state that since they believe Bible prophecy is unknowable, therefore students of God's Word might better spend their time on "more profitable studies," such as personal sanctification, evangelism, and other weighty matters. But the study of prophecy must be profitable, or why would God have placed it prominently throughout His Word? Throughout the New Testament we are called to watch and wait for the Lord's return.

In the New Testament, one verse in thirty is concerned with the Second Coming of Jesus Christ.[1] Jesus Himself constantly referred to prophecy. At one point after His Resurrection He explained to two of His disciples that He had fulfilled all the Messianic prophecies (Luke 24:44, 45).

Yet today many people still say we shouldn't waste our time on prophecy because prophecy is unknowable. What a colossal cop-out!

There's no doubt that Bible prophecy *is* extremely difficult to understand—although it will get easier as we near the time of the end (Daniel 12:9, 10). However, we shouldn't relegate it to the trash basket. As we see the world falling apart in so many ways, as we see the rise of false teachers and cults throughout the world, coupled with growing apostasy within the church, and as a world political pattern emerges that was clearly forecast thousands of years ago in God's Word, we should be spending *more*—not less—of our time studying Bible prophecy.

True, many points of Bible prophecy *are* open to question and varying interpretations, and true, many reckless people *have* mishandled prophecy, but that shouldn't deflect us from seriously, yet humbly studying the topic.

History From God's Point of View

In many ways the entire Bible is prophecy. Wasn't the first promise God made to Adam and Eve after the fall a prophecy? Wasn't every sacrifice from the time of Abel presented to God through faith in the word of prophecy?[2] Arthur E. Bloomfield explains:

> God had something in mind—a very definite goal—when He created the world. All the Bible points toward that goal. It is the development of one master plan. It always looks ahead. In that sense, the entire Bible is prophecy. A study of prophecy is a study of the Bible. A study of the Bible without the prophetic forward look is merely a study of certain aspects of history. Prophecy is history from God's viewpoint.[3]

In James J. Brookes's 1878 book, *Maranatha or the Lord Cometh,* he gave an impassioned argument for studying Bible prophecy:

> The historical books of the Old Testament are radiant with the light of prophecy. A very considerable proportion of the Psalms is entirely occupied with prophecy. The whole of the Scriptures from Isaiah to Malachi consists of prophecy. The ministry of John the

> Baptist was absorbed with prophecy. The discourses of our Lord are filled with prophecy. All the leading Epistles of the New Testament contain prophecy, and the last book of the Bible is prophecy throughout.
>
> What then do these thoughtless persons mean by their inconsiderate objections to the study of prophecy? Do they not know that if they tear prophecy out of the Scriptures it is like tearing the warp out of the woof, and leaving only shapeless shreds of truth? Do they not know that prophecy, expressed or implied, is found in almost every chapter of the Bible?[4]

Most compelling about anyone's study of Bible prophecy is that we're not dealing with what the Hebrew prophets have said *might* happen. We're dealing with what absolutely *will* happen someday. The separation point between all of history's psychics and the biblical prophets—Jeremiah, Moses, Isaiah, Daniel, and others—is that everything the Hebrew prophets forecast for the future has come true with 100 percent accuracy, except for a remarkably unified set of events they spoke of for the "latter days" or the time of the end. How can we fail to believe that these, too, will come to pass?

Old Testament Prophecies

One of the interesting things about Hal Lindsey's *The Late Great Planet Earth* is that he pointed out in a popular fashion how deadly accurate the Hebrew prophets were. Jeremiah, for example, stated that Judah, the southern kingdom of Israel, would be invaded and destroyed by the king of Babylon and that its people would be carried off to Babylon as slaves and that they would remain there for seventy years (Jeremiah 25:9–11). Although Jeremiah was persecuted for his bad tidings, a short time later it happened exactly as he said it would.[5]

Lindsey then recounts the story recorded in 1 Kings 22 of a little-known prophet named Micaiah, who told King

Ahab that he would be killed in battle and that the Israeli army would be routed. After Micaiah called four hundred of Ahab's soothsayers liars, because they had told the king he would win the battle, the ruler imprisoned the prophet. Not wanting to take chances, though, he went to battle disguised and wearing armor. An enemy archer fulfilled the prophet's words when he shot an arrow during battle, and it struck Ahab in a small, exposed place in his armor, killing him. The Israeli army was routed.[6]

Isaiah accurately predicted that Jerusalem would be spared a defeat and King Sennacherib would be killed by the sword (Isaiah 36, 37); he prophesied 100 years into the future, saying Babylon would completely destroy Judah and carry away Israel's treasures (Isaiah 39:5–7); he prophesied 150 years in the future, by predicting Babylon would be conquered by the Medes (Isaiah 13:17–22); and he prophesied 200 years in the future, when he foresaw a king named Cyrus would see that Jerusalem and the temple were rebuilt (Isaiah 44:28–45:4).[7]

There are many more examples of the Hebrew prophets accurately foretelling God's future plans. But some of the most exciting prophecies foretold God's sending of His Promised One, the Messiah of Israel. When Jesus came the first time, He fulfilled about three hundred specific Old Testament prophecies.[8]

Prophecies Concerning Christ's First Coming

Consider a few of the prophecies Christ fulfilled in His coming:

In the Garden of Eden, God told Adam and Eve that in the future the seed of a woman would bruise Satan's head.	Genesis 3:15

The prophet Nathan predicted someone from King David's line would become God's Promised One: . . . "I will establish his throne forever. I will be his father, and he will be my son. I will never take my love away from him . . . . I will set him over my house and my kingdom forever; his throne will be established forever."	1 Chronicles 17:12–14
He was a descendant of David according to His mother's lineage.	Luke 1:27
He was descended from David on the side of His earthly father.	Matthew 1:6, 16
He would be like Moses, and God would require everyone to listen to His words.	Deuteronomy 18:18, 19
He would be born in Bethlehem.	Micah 5:2
He would be born of a virgin.	Isaiah 7:14
A messenger would precede Him.	Malachi 3:1; Isaiah 40:3
He would open the eyes of the blind and heal the deaf, dumb and lame.	Isaiah 35:4–6
He would come into Jerusalem on a donkey.	Zechariah 9:9
He would be betrayed for thirty pieces of silver.	Psalm 41:9; Zechariah 11:12

He would be beaten and killed.	Isaiah 53; Psalm 22
He would be pierced.	Zechariah 12:10
Some would gamble for His garments.	Psalm 22:18
Not a bone of His body would be broken.	Numbers 9:12
He would be buried by a rich man.	Isaiah 53:9
He would be resurrected.	Psalm 16:9, 10; 21:4

On the basis of that, can we say God has been any less specific about his prophecies concerning the last days?

The Return of the Jews Prophesied

As intriguing as the prophecies of Jesus' coming is the Hebrew prophets' foretelling of the return of the Jews to Palestine "in the latter days," after their worldwide dispersion. This prophecy was fulfilled in 1948, when Israel became a nation, and since that time, Israel has prospered and grown, even taking the old city of Jerusalem during the six-day war in 1967. More prophecies about Israel in the "latter days" are continuing to be fulfilled.

For centuries many scholars scoffed at the idea of the Jews returning to their homeland and becoming a nation again. They ignored the clear teachings of Scripture—and the teachings of Jesus Himself—when they denied Israel would be reborn. (It is indeed interesting that Jesus said, ". . . Jerusalem will be trampled on by the Gentiles until the times of the Gentiles are fulfilled" [Luke 21:24].) Because of the lie called "replacement theology," which zoomed into prominence in the Middle Ages, some believed the Jews would not return to their homeland. This idea says God is through with Israel forever and that He replaced her with the church.

But throughout history, some studious men and women

divided the Word of God carefully and knew God's promises to Israel were meant to last forever. Long before Jewish settlers began to trickle back into Palestine, James J. Brookes wrote that although the idea of the country being reborn "will seem very absurd to those who 'look on things after the outward appearance,' "[9] God's promises to bring back the Jews were "absolutely unconditional."[10]

Let's look at some of the prophecies involving the return of the Jews to Palestine in the latter days.

> In that day the Lord will reach out his hand a second time to reclaim the remnant that is left of his people from Assyria, from Lower Egypt, from Upper Egypt, from Cush, from Elam, from Babylonia, from Hamath and from the islands of the sea.
>
> Isaiah 11:11
>
> The Lord will have compassion on Jacob; once again he will choose Israel and will settle them in their own land. . . .
>
> Isaiah 14:1

Later Isaiah says that when Israel is restored to Palestine, the once-desolate land will blossom with flowers and the desert will become green (Isaiah 35:1, 2). Anyone who has been to Israel recently will know that prophecy has been fulfilled. Israel, once thought to be a desolate, arid country, has become one of the leading citrus producers in the world, due to the miracle of irrigation.

One of the most illustrative passages dealing with the return of the Jews to Palestine is found in Ezekiel 37. It is the story of "Dem bones, Dem bones, Dem dry bones," as the classic spiritual goes. God explains the point of the bones coming to life again: " '. . . I will bring you back to the land of Israel. . . . I will settle you in your own land. Then you will know that I the Lord have spoken, and have done it, declares the Lord' " (Ezekiel 37:12, 14).

Other passages dealing with the return of the Jews to their homeland are found in Zechariah 12; Jeremiah 30; Zephaniah 3; and Micah 7:11–13. The Micah passage has an ominous ring to it. It says when the Jews return, the whole earth will be judged and "become desolate" because of the deeds of men. Jeremiah backs that up by saying it will be the time of "trouble for Jacob . . . How awful that day will be! None will be like it" (30:7).

Christ's Second Coming Prophesied

"Among the early Christians there was, perhaps, no doctrine that was more the object of firm belief, and the ground of more delightful contemplation, than that their ascended Master would return."[11] Perhaps they believed it so firmly because the Second Coming of Christ is one of the most frequent prophecies in the Bible, mentioned more than five hundred times.[12]

New Testament Prophecy. In the Upper Room, when the disciples became distraught because Jesus was leaving, He comforted them, " 'Do not let your hearts be troubled. . . . I will come back and take you to be with me . . .' " (John 14:1, 3).

After the Ascension, the disciples stood gazing up into the skies, but two angels told them, " '. . . This same Jesus . . . will come back in the same way you have seen him go into heaven' " (Acts 1:11).

In one of Paul's last epistles, the Apostle says, "We wait for the blessed hope—the glorious appearing of our great God and Savior, Jesus Christ" (Titus 2:13).

The Apostle John wrote, ". . . When he appears, we shall be like him, for we shall see him as he is. Everyone who has this hope in him purifies himself . . ." (1 John 3:2, 3). The "blessed hope" of Christians throughout the centuries has been rooted in the realization that Jesus *is* coming back. That fact is repeated over and over across the New Testament pages.

The New Testament discloses some other things about the Second Coming. In Matthew 24, Luke 21, and Mark 13 Jesus Himself gave extensive details of how the world would look when He comes back. His "signs of the times" look strangely like twentieth-century earth. He described the signs as nation rising up against nation, famines and earthquakes, religious persecution, and a great falling away from the true faith. Religious deception is the biggest sign to look for, according to Matthew 24. Three separate times (vv. 5, 11, and 23, 24), He tells His disciples to watch out for false prophets and people claiming to be the Christ.

Old Testament Prophecy. In the Old Testament the Second Coming of Christ was often referred to as the "Day of the Lord." Daniel writes of ". . . one like a son of man, coming with the clouds of heaven . . ." (Daniel 7:13).

Zechariah writes of the Messiah's return to destroy Israel's enemies:

> "On that day I will set out to destroy all the nations that attack Jerusalem, And I will pour out on the house of David and the inhabitants of Jerusalem a spirit of grace and supplication. They will look on me, the one they have pierced. . . ."
>
> Zechariah 12:9, 10

There is no question that the greatest prophecy of both testaments yet to be fulfilled is the return of Jesus Christ.

Early Christians frequently prayed *Maranatha,* "Come, Lord Jesus." And the Bible ends with the promise, "He who testifies to these things says, 'Yes, I am coming soon . . .' " (Revelation 22:20).

To which the believing church responds, ". . . Amen. Come, Lord Jesus" (Revelation 22:20).

5
Repent, the End Is Near!

The Apostle Paul had reason for concern when he wrote his second letter to the Thessalonian congregation. Mainly he admonished the congregation to stick to what they'd already been told about the Second Coming of Christ and not believe in false apocalyptic reports:

> Concerning the coming of our Lord Jesus Christ and our being gathered to him, we ask you, brothers, not to become easily unsettled or alarmed by some prophecy, report or letter supposed to have come from us, saying that the day of the Lord has already come. Don't let anyone deceive you in any way, for that day will not come until the rebellion occurs and the man of lawlessness is revealed, the man doomed to destruction. He opposes and exalts himself over everything that is called God or is worshiped, and even sets himself up in God's temple, proclaiming himself to be God.
>
> 2 Thessalonians 2:1–4

In the next verse he added: "Don't you remember that when I was with you I used to tell you these things?"

The Thessalonian Christians had apparently heard wild

rumors that the Second Coming of Christ had already come. Some had even given up their jobs and were sponging off the other brethren. But Paul blasted them, told them to get busy, and proclaimed: ". . . If a man will not work, he shall not eat" (3:10).

The situation at Thessalonica was not an aberration. Similar end-time themes—rumors of the Lord's soon return, the battle of Armageddon, the rise of the Antichrist—have cropped up throughout church history. In every case and in every generation we have found that if we followed Paul's admonition—for believers to stick with what they've been told (through God's Word) and to keep busy—we would have stopped frenzied end-time fever dead in its tracks. For most end-time movements, as we shall see, have ended in disappointment for—and sometimes embarrassment to—genuine believers in Christ. They have also often caused the true gospel to become discredited. For although many end-time movements or millennial movements were pseudo-Christian or non-Christian cultic movements, others have swept away thousands of God-fearing, Bible-believing Christians.

According to Norman Cohn, well-meaning religious folks have never had trouble finding the "signs of the times" in contemporary events:

> People were always on the watch for the "signs" which, according to the prophetic tradition, were to herald and accompany the final "time of troubles"; and since the "signs" included bad rulers, civil discord, war, drought, famine, plague, comets, sudden deaths of prominent persons and an increase in general sinfulness, there was never any difficulty about finding them. Invasion or the threat of invasion by Huns, Magyars, Mongols, Saracens or Turks always stirred memories of those hordes of Antichrist, the people of Gog and Magog. Above all, any ruler who could be regarded as a tyrant was apt to take on the features of Antichrist. . . .[1]

Let's look at some of the other times when Christians became alarmed by the thought that the end was upon them.

A.D. 156—The Montanist Movement of Phrygia. Phrygia was an ancient country of west-central Asia Minor (now Turkey), settled in the thirteenth century B.C. Following Christ's resurrection, the gospel had great success there and in other parts of Asia Minor; and John's Revelation was written to seven churches in Asia Minor.

But in A.D. 156 a man named Montanus arose and declared himself to be the "Spirit of Truth"—the incarnation of the Holy Spirit, mentioned in John's Gospel, which was to reveal things to come. The movement quickly caught on as a number of people (today we might call them hypercharismatics) began gathering around Montanus, claiming divinely originated ecstatic experiences and visions.

Their revelations (which they began calling "the Third Testament") told them the kingdom of God was coming soon and that the New Jerusalem would soon descend from heaven and land in central Turkey, where it would become home for all the saints. The visionaries quickly sent word out to all Christians, summoning them to Phrygia to wait for the Second Coming.[2]

Strangely even though the New Jerusalem never materialized, the Montanist movement grew. Some of its followers were even martyred for their beliefs. Noted Cohn:

> [It] . . . spread far and wide, not only through Asia Minor but to Africa, Rome and even Gaul [Spain]. Although Montanists no longer looked to Phrygia, their confidence in the imminent appearance of the New Jerusalem was unshaken; and this was true even for Tertullian, the most famous theologian in the West at that time, when he joined the movement.[3]

The movement divided Christians into camps of those who believed in the soon appearance of the New Jerusalem and those who didn't—continuous strife resulted. Finally the organized church acted. In 431 the Council of Ephesus condemned belief in the millennium as a superstitious aberration.[4] But this really didn't put an end to it, according to Cohn. Traces of the movement could even be seen nine centuries later, in the Crusades, as the advancing armies of Europeans claimed to have seen the heavenly Jerusalem in the sky about to descend.[5]

A.D. 1000—A Doomsday Explosion. In some ways the approach of the year A.D. 1000 was a lot like today, as we approach the year 2000. Then, as now, we have an explosion of doomsday sentiments. However, the last time around, the Roman Catholic Church stirred it up. Around the year 900, an ecumenical council of the Roman Catholic Church declared that the final century of history had begun, the world was in its "last days," and Christ would return around the year 1000 and usher in the Golden Age.

"Intense excitement prevailed throughout a large part of Europe." They believed that Christ would return at the end of the "first thousand years of the Christian era. . . . Multitudes sold their estates to unbelievers and gave away the proceeds in charities, business was neglected, the fields were left uncultivated, and for some years the wildest confusion and terror reigned."[6]

But Jesus failed to return when expected.

A.D. 1186—The Third Crusade and the Letter of Toledo. A great deal of end-time fever accompanied the launching of the third crusade, especially in England. Prophecies, believed to have been penned by astrologers in Spain, began circulating in 1184, telling of a new world order. Then in 1186 a "Letter of Toledo" circulated throughout Europe, instructing everyone to hide in caves and mountains, because the world was about to be devastated by wind and storm, drought and famine, pestilence and earthquake. Only a faithful remnant of Christians would be spared, the letter declared.[7]

However, life went on.

A.D. 1260—Brother Arnold, Friend of the Poor. Brother Arnold, a dissident Dominican monk, wrote a manifesto in Swabia. He said that in a short time—in 1260—the end of the era and the start of a new age would begin. He was typical of soothsayers from the eleventh century to the sixteenth century, because the desires of the poor to improve their lot in life colored his last-days scenario. In his scheme of things, just prior to 1260 he would call upon Christ, in the name of the poor, to judge the pope and church leaders. Christ would respond to his call and would appear on the earth to pronounce His judgment and to reveal the pope as the Antichrist and the clergy as limbs of the Antichrist.[8]

He gained a large following among the poor, but his manifesto never panned out.

A.D. 1420—Martinek Hauska Says the Fire Will Come Down. In 1420, near the city of Prague, a number of disgruntled priests, led by Martinek Hauska, banded together to herald the Second Coming of Christ. They told everyone to hide in the mountains, because between February 1 and February 14, 1420, God would destroy every town and village with fire and usher in the millennium. Wrote Cohn: "Throughout Christendom the wrath of God would overtake everyone who did not at once flee to 'the mountains'—which were defined as five particular towns in Bohemia, all of them Taborite strongholds."[9] Hauska's followers then went on a rampage to "purify the earth" by killing their enemies—the clergy of the day.

Fire never fell.

A.D. 1527—A Nutty Bookbinder. In 1527, a German bookbinder named, appropriately enough, Hans Nut declared himself a prophet and announced that he had been sent by Christ to herald His coming, which Nut said was slated for 1528. His arrival would be followed by a thousand years of free food, love, and free sex.[10] Obviously, it didn't happen. Nut was captured in 1527 and killed during an Augsburg prison escape attempt, but he did amass some followers in southern Germany.[11]

A.D. 1533 and 1534. Will the Anabaptists' New Jerusalem Be in Strassburg or Münster? The Anabaptist movement of the early 1500s reeked with end-time fever. One Anabaptist writer issued a prophecy that the millennium would begin in 1533 and that Strassburg (today called Strasbourg, France) had been chosen by God as the New Jerusalem. Out from Strassburg would flow God's Spirit so that no one on earth would be able to resist it—or stop the saints' wonder-working power. The two witnesses, Enoch and Elijah, would also appear and destroy the unbelieving earth.[12]

When the prophecy failed, the Anabaptists became more zealous and claimed that two witnesses *had* come in the form of Jan Matthys and Jan Bockelson; they would set up the New Jerusalem in Münster. Münster became a frightening dictatorship under Bockelson's control.

Although all Lutherans and Catholics were expelled from that city, the millennium never came.

The French Prophets of the Early 1700s. The Camisards were an eighteenth-century French group that prophesied in ecstatic trances and spoke in tongues, foretelling the imminent destruction of the Roman Catholic Church, which they referred to as Babylon and Satan. But things got hot for them, and they fled to England, where they began issuing similar condemnations against the church in London. Known in England as the "French Prophets" and for their prophecies of destruction and a new world to come, they attained a large following and worldwide attention. When their prophecies failed to materialize, a rapid decline in membership followed. However, the Shakers, a group that attained a following in America, is said to have stemmed from the Camisard movement.[13]

A.D. 1844—The Millerite Movement. The major doomsday miscalculation in the Western Hemisphere occurred in

1844, in upstate New York, with a group founded by William Miller, known as "the Millerites," or "the Adventists." The movement had begun years earlier, when Miller announced, after an intensive study of the Scriptures, "I am fully convinced that sometime between March 21, 1843, and March 21, 1844 . . . Christ will come and bring all His saints with Him, and then He will reward every man as His work shall be."

At first, some of Miller's associates were skeptical of his date. So a conference was called in the spring of 1942, in Boston, to talk about the date of the end.[14] The result was a resolution telling Jesus when He would be returning, according to the June 1, 1842, issue of the *Signs of the Times*, an official organ of the movement: "RESOLVED, that in the opinion of this conference, there are most serious and important reasons for believing that God has revealed the time of the end of the world, and that that time is 1843."

As the magic date approached, Miller had gained over 50,000 followers, many of whom sold all their property, refused to plow their fields, and gave away all their possessions, "For surely the Lord will return before another winter." Journalists reported on Millerites who had climbed to the tops of trees and then tried, presumably unsuccessfully, to take off for heaven to meet Christ. Thousands of the faithful gathered on hilltops to wait for the Lord.[15] According to a 1924 book about the movement, the Millerites made for colorful newspaper copy:

> The world made merry over the old prophet's predicament. The taunts and jeers of the "scoffers" were well-nigh unbearable. If any of Miller's followers walked abroad, they ran the gauntlet of merciless ridicule.
>
> "What!—not gone up yet?—We thought you'd gone up! Aren't you going up soon?—Wife didn't go up and leave you behind to burn, did she?"
>
> The rowdy element in the community would not leave them alone.[16]

After Jesus failed to show, the Millerites tried setting new dates for the Lord's coming. But following their fourth new date—October 22, 1844—the movement collapsed. Miller, who meanwhile had been excommunicated from a Baptist church in New York, eventually publicly acknowledged his mistake and never set a new one. He died five years later, a humbled man.

Since those days, many other end-of-the-world movements have come and gone. Some of them have been spurred on by cult groups such as the Jehovah's Witnesses, who have predicted the battle of Armageddon in 1914, 1915, 1918, 1923, 1925, and 1975. The Children of God (Family of Love), who claim their leader, David Berg, is "God's end-time prophet to the world," fled America en masse in 1973, due to Berg's pronouncement that Comet Kohoutek would destroy America.

How Did Believers Enter This Game?

Still, many of the rash predictions and prophecies of the end times have come from Christians—not cultists. How did they get involved in such things?

Maybe it's because Christians often feel overwhelmed by the wickedness of a fallen world. Since Scripture describes the end times as having great evil, political disorder, and religious apostasy, believers may assume *they* live in the most morally dark era, so theirs must be the last one.

John described the age we live in as "the last hour" (1 John 2:18) and warned people about the spirit of the antichrist. Jesus told the disciples they would "hear of wars and rumors of wars" (Matthew 24:5). In periods of troubles—political, social, and religious unrest—as the pressure on those who want to follow God faithfully rises, they naturally look to Him. Some look to Him for help amid their troubles; others look for a purely miraculous way out of their problems.

In A.D. 1000, plenty of people would have liked a way out

of their hard spots. Europe swelled with political changes, and unrest existed in most countries in the early part of the eleventh century. England would be conquered by the Danes, ending the haphazard rule of Aethelred the Unready; in France the Capetian kings were having trouble with their vassals; and the Holy Roman Empire was far from peaceful.

At the same time the papacy was weakening. Not too much on the political or religious scene looked good to many believers, and it would have been nice to have Jesus take them all away from it.

As the papacy began to gain political and religious power in the Middle Ages, the pope became a popular candidate in the Antichrist-naming game. People of that period did not have a hard time seeing how such a leader could fit into an end-times scheme. The pope became a powerful leader, who not only held the reins of the church, but could sway leaders with the threat of excommunication. Once a king was barred from the church, all his vassals could more or less legally take up arms against him.

When popes acted in a less than spiritual fashion—and many had greater interests in their worldly powers than the spiritual ones—it's easy to understand why people would begin to seek the return of Jesus. In fact, many did.

Is It Any Different in Our Time?

What of the soothsayers today? Are they different from the others we've looked at?

We live in a time of massive change, when many are looking for a simpler way of living—trying to return to the past to recapture an elusive stability. Maybe our television and radio teachers who predict the Second Advent have simply given a new twist to an old doomsday message. Like the soothsayers of other ages, they have failed and have produced scoffers, who ridicule the Lord's promise to return.

But why so *many* soothsayers now? Perhaps it is because we live in an age that has seen:

1. The establishing of the state of Israel, which has given Jews a homeland that they control for the first time since Old Testament days. This is an apparent fulfillment of prophecy (Isaiah 14:1).
2. The rise of the European Economic Community (EEC), also known as the European Common Market, which some students of prophecy believe may eventually fulfill Daniel 7:19–24.
3. The approach of the year 2000, which, like the year 1000, brings millennial speculation out of the woodwork.

Yet these reasons do not give any Christian the right to go beyond what Scripture says, and they certainly don't give anyone the authority to contradict Scripture.

No one knows the ". . . times or dates the Father has set by his own authority" (Acts 1:7). It's about time today's students of prophecy keep busy with the work of the kingdom, holding fast *only* to what God has told us through His Word about events leading to the Second Advent. The many clear signs of the times should impel us to do His work, not waste effort timing the exact day of His coming.

The Lord does not set His return to suit anyone's schedule. But even the scoffers need to realize that His delay evidences His grace. For: "The Lord is not slow in keeping his promise, as some understand slowness. He is patient with you, not wanting anyone to perish, but everyone to come to repentance" (2 Peter 3:9).

Neither will Christians have any reason to be ashamed if we have remained faithful to the work He has set before us to accomplish.

He *could* come today!

Part II
Who's Afraid of the Big, Bad Wolf?

Take a look at some of the amazing ideas that make up so many of the end-times soothsayers' predictions:

- An alignment of the planets will signify the end of man.
- A computer-system beast will rule the earth's economy.
- The number of the beast, 666, can be seen in the Apollo space mission, Israeli lottery tickets, and major credit cards—to name only a few sources.
- South American killer bees will be the fulfillment of the fifth trumpet predicted in Revelation—they are the "locusts" of the end times.

It almost seems as if such prognosticators look under every rock for another sign of our modern age to add to the biblical record, and anything they can force into their own vision of Revelation seems to become a part of the fearful doomsday message.

Doubtless many of the fear mongers have been tremendously successful. You can see it in the sales of their books and tapes and the money that willing hands pour into their ministries. Such success seems to feed on people's desire to hear something new and terrifying, just the way you liked to go see scary movies when you were a child.

It's not as if the Bible didn't have some terrifying news to report of the end times:

- Hail and fire mixed with blood will fall on the earth, destroying one-third of the vegetation (Revelation 8:7).
- One-third of the sea will turn to blood (Revelation 8:8).
- One-third of mankind will be destroyed (Revelation 9:15–18).
- Those who follow the Antichrist will have painful sores break out all over their bodies (Revelation 16:2).
- Everything in the sea will die, and rivers and springs will be destroyed (Revelation 16:3, 4).

Somehow, in the face of all that, many modern-day predictions seem a bit small. But more than that, if you look at the words of these doomsday prophets, add a smidgeon of scientific knowledge and logic, and consider them in light of the Word, the prophecies almost seem to debunk themselves. It's time to look at what they are saying—and put such teachings under the clear light of commonsense teaching.

6
I Love a Parade

> The prediction is that San Francisco, Los Angeles and surrounding areas wil be lost in the coming earthquakes triggered by celestial phenomena in 1982. Is it possible that several million people will die in the fires or in the watery graves predicted to transpire that year? . . . Could millions in New York City perish should that city be affected like San Francisco was in 1906?[1]

In 1976 prophecy teacher Doug Clark was writing about a strange alignment of all nine planets in the solar system, called the Jupiter Effect, that was scheduled to take place in 1982. Warning his growing audience about coming destruction, he also gave practical advice: Flee from the coastlands, store food, sell your homes and your stocks, and don't place your savings in banks located in the earthquake or low-lying belts.[2]

Not many people followed Clark's advice, but one thing is certain: He did foresee in the Jupiter Effect the beginning of the apocalypse. After the Jupiter Effect sparked worldwide destruction, he said things would continue going downhill. "By 1985, we are going to have a food war."[3] A new money system was on its way, and "West Germany is now stamping people's hands, according to reliable sources, and this is very, very close to the description of the Mark of the Beast outlined in the Bible. . . . Never take the mark on the back of your hand!"[4]

Then he made a startling statement: Jesus would return in 1982:

> Today as we watch all these signs in the skies, we rejoice because we know these mysteries will soon be revealed to us. *Perhaps in 1982, these mysteries of life will be known to us when Jesus returns to Earth to fulfill his teachings and elevate man to a higher level of being.*[5]

Today Clark, who hosts "Shockwaves of Armageddon," a weekly television show on the Trinity Broadcasting Network, is somewhat embarrassed about the book in which he wrote these things. But he says he has learned from it.

The Start of the Parade

For the record, the Jupiter Effect, or the "parade of planets," came and went as it does every 179 years, and the world kept on as always, without a single major quake in southern California. But in defense of Clark, he wasn't the only one to predict catastrophe in 1982. In fact, many dispensational prophecy teachers did in the late 1970s or early 1980s. Perhaps they had fair reason to: They were scared into it by two astronomy experts, John R. Gribbin and Stephen Plagemann, authors of *The Jupiter Effect*.

Their book predicted massive worldwide destruction caused by the alignment—especially in southern California. The alignment "points to 1982 as the year in which the Los Angeles region of the San Andreas fault will be subjected to the most massive earthquake known in the populated regions of the Earth in this century. . . . Los Angeles will be destroyed."[6] Perhaps prophecy teachers erred in accepting this imminent disaster because they did not recognize what the astronomical community at large was saying about the Jupiter Effect. Although Gribbin and Plagemann had their fans, many scientists pooh-poohed their predictions.

Nevertheless some big names in evangelicalism jumped on the Jupiter Effect bandwagon, describing the disasters it would cause. In a long-playing record that accompanied Hal Lindsey's book *The 1980's: Countdown to Armageddon,* Lindsey said he believed the Jupiter Effect, which he likened to "signs in the sun, moon and stars" mentioned in Luke 21:25 could cause "five or six meltdowns" at nuclear power plants:

> According to Dr. Plagemann it will be "the last straw." There are dams built on the faults and nuclear power plants on the faults. Could there be five or six meltdowns?
>
> It will slow the rotation of the earth down where the crust will go through great stress and there will be great earthquakes and a reaction of dormant volcanos. . . . If these scientists are right, then what we can expect in 1982 we'll have the largest outbreak of killer quakes ever seen in the history of planet earth along with radical changes in climate and most climatologists believe that the shift is already taking place.[7]

Similarly, Christian broadcaster Pat Robertson wrote that the Jupiter Effect may be tied in with a Russian invasion of Israel, as prophesied in Ezekiel 38. "All available economic and military intelligence pinpoints 1982 as the optimum time for such a Soviet strike," Robertson wrote. "Ezekiel indicates enormous earthquake activity and severe hailstones in Israel at the time of the predicted Russian invasion. . . . According to these scientists [Gribbin and Plagemann], in 1982 there will be an alignment of planets on the same side of the sun which will exert a sufficiently strong additional gravitational pull on the earth to cause disruptions in the earth's upper atmosphere, radical changes in climatic conditions (hailstones?), and severe earthquakes."[8]

But none of them outdid the Southwest Radio Church on the Jupiter Effect phenomenon. In newsletters, booklets, and during its worldwide daily broadcasts, the Oklahoma City based ministry repeatedly talked about the "Parade of Planets," from 1974 right up until 1982. Dr. Emil Gaverluk, writing in the ministry's the *Gospel Truth* newsletter, in 1979, had the parade possibly throwing Mars out of its orbit and plunging toward earth! "This is hard to believe," wrote Gaverluk, but it could happen.[9]

David Webber and Noah Hutchings of the Southwest Radio Church hinted that the rapture of the church might occur before the parade of planets and that the celestial event could result in "the earth [being] righted on its axis and pre-Flood conditions restored."[10] They also noted that the Jupiter Effect could cause the earthquakes associated with the great tribulation, mentioned in the book of Revelation. Referring people to Ezekiel 38:20 and Revelation 16:19–21, they, too, had heeded the theories of Gribbin and Plagemann.[11]

But strangely enough, after nothing out of the ordinary happened in 1982, the Jupiter Effect was scarcely mentioned again by the Southwest Radio Church. Nor was there an apology. When asked why, in a recent interview, Hutchings conceded that the Jupiter Effect was not what he and others thought it would be. He did insist, though, that some disasters such as the eruption of Mount Saint Helens, in Washington, were caused by the planets.[12]

Charles Taylor and Colin Deal were others who thought the alignment of planets was a portent of the end.

But some prophecy teachers had second thoughts about the apocalyptic-sounding reports of potential disaster. They began backing off the Jupiter Effect teachings. In James McKeever's August, 1980, edition of *Christians Will Go Through the Tribulation,* he talked about potential disaster in California due to the alignment.[13] But a year later in his newsletter he ran a reprint of an article critical of the Jupiter Effect.[14]

Others, such as Clark, who were fooled by Gribbin and Plagemann's sensational projections, have learned from it. Clark said he's learned not to set dates from the experience. Here's what he has to say about it today:

> Yes, that was a mistake on my part, an honest mistake because I did feel the alignment of the planets could tie in to some sort of cataclysmic type event. Number two, I was wrong. Number three, I don't pick dates on anything anymore, and I don't look into these physical things as having direct imminency on the coming of the Lord. . . . I'm a lot more careful. I think we all make one or two major mistakes.[15]

We might profit greatly from his hindsight.

What Does Science Say?

While some were looking to the stars and planets for confirmation of the Second Coming, most scientists went along with business as usual. Perhaps some were not trying to ignore God or His Word—they had just seen enough of His creation that they knew what to expect. The "portents" others saw were nothing new in the scientific world.

For example, Frank Maloney, an associate professor of astronomy and astrophysics at Villanova University, says the public overlooks some of the most prominent comets. He remembers seeing comet West in 1976 with the naked eye, and he remembers Bennett's comet, a prominent yellowish comet that appeared in 1970.

According to the book *Comets—The Swords of Heaven,* West was "one of the most spectacular comets ever seen." But it was "virtually unnoticed by the public on its 1976 visit, because Comet Kohoutek in 1973 had turned out to be much less glorious than expected, and so the mass media gave Comet West little publicity."[16]

Why bring up these fly-by visitors from outer space? Because many of today's soothsayers of the Second Advent are looking to the comets as "proof" that God is setting up the final end-time events. Some have cited Halley's comet of 1986 and Kohoutek of 1973 as heralds of the time of the end. These soothsayers argue that the comets are signs—similar to astrological portents—from God to warn us of future events. The significance applied to the last passing of Halley's comet varies among prophecy teachers. In 1981 Mary Stewart Relfe suggested that Halley's comet may "be given the most distinguished honor yet, heralding the LORD OF LORDS AND KING OF KINGS! Even so come, Lord Jesus!"[17] But Colin Deal suggested that the comet could "pronounce the death of another Roman emperor [antichrist],"[18] while Chuck Smith[19] and James McKeever both suggested its coming could be an important last-day sign in the heavens. McKeever even hinted "God could intervene and change its elliptical orbit to achieve some of His purposes" in the last days.[20] Last, Constance Cumbey wrote of a plot to reveal the New Age messiah (Antichrist) in Israel before the arrival of Halley's comet early in 1986.[21]

The reason for bringing an astronomy professor into this is that both Halley's and Kohoutek's recent visits were not very noteworthy when compared with other recent comets. If comets *do* signify major world events about to happen, as many soothsayers claim, what noteworthy events did these comets—widely known to astronomers—reveal? Most of them were far brighter than Halley's or Kohoutek:

Arend-Roland (1957)
Humason (1962)
Ikeya (1963)
Ikeya-Seki (1965)
Mitchell-Jone-Gerber (1967)
Mrkos (1957)
Seki-Lines (1962)
Tago-Sato-Kosaka (1969)

The truth of the matter is, as any astronomer wil tell you, the appearance of comets has nothing to do with earthly events such as the overthrow of governments or the death of world leaders. Instead, astronomers say mankind's centuries-old myths about comets work the other way around. Since there are always so many comets coming around the sun, one can always attribute a war or death to a comet.

"Comets are coming in all the time," says Maloney. "On the average a half a dozen new ones are coming in every year. And the rate has remained unchanged in the past 120–130 years. They're not coming in any faster in the past several decades."[22]

Despite the clear evidence about comets' frequency, some of today's Christian soothsayers still encourage their listeners to search for meanings on the tail of the comet. David Webber, for example, suggests that Halley's comet could have been the star of Bethlehem that led the wise men to baby Jesus, and if it could be proven that it was so, we could "declare with supreme confidence THE SECOND COMING OF CHRIST IS NEAR, even at the door."[23]

Webber and Noah Hutchings also stated that Kohoutek was not the dud of the century, as many thought. It was the herald of United States President Nixon's ouster and the fall of many other leaders:

> Within the year, all nine leaders of the Common Market nations of Europe, and President Nixon of the United States, comprising the leaders of all nations recognized in the so-called free world, fell, through death or political disgrace.
>
> . . . Even though Kohoutek may have been a scientific fizzle, its prophetic mission to foretell the doom of rulers was an amazing success.[24]

What lies behind various prophetic ministries urging people to look at signs in space? It's hard to tell for sure. Evidently some ministries promote a form of "Christian" astrology and interpretation of omens, despite the fact both practices are strongly condemned in God's Word (Deuteronomy 18:10; Isaiah 48:13, 14). When we look toward the stars and planets, let us keep in mind that it is God who created them (Genesis 1; Psalm 8:3), and though we may study them, they should not govern our lives. Only God's Word can do that!

7
The Beast of Brussels and the New Money System

Colin Deal thought he was on to something in 1979. In his book, *Christ Returns by 1988—101 Reasons Why,* he wrote that one of the leading economic forecasters in the United States predicted that a total collapse of the dollar "could take place as early as October 15, 1980. . . . How soon? I am not positive. That it will happen though, I am positive. The tribulation is almost here!"[1]

He further talked about the collapse of the dollar and soon arrival of a new money system that could eventually lead to the Antichrist's cashless society, foretold in the Bible: "He also forced everyone, small and great, rich and poor, free and slave, to receive a mark on his right hand or on his forehead, so that no one could buy or sell unless he had the mark, which is the name of the beast or the number of his name" (Revelation 13:16, 17).

Deal, in fact, suggested something a bit more ominous: The United States government had already started to mint a new coin to replace the dollar, which might place the nation on the road to holocaust. The culprit was the new—and now nearly out of circulation—Susan B. Anthony coin. "Will this coin signal the end . . . Will it also signal the beginning of a 'new (world) order of the ages' as predicted by John (Revelation 13)?" asked Deal. "Watch for the replacement of the American dollar and its symbolic meaning. Isn't it odd that this new coin, minted in a God-fearing nation, has the bust of Susan B. Anthony, a renowned atheist and the instigator of the present unrest with women's liberation?"[2]

Today we can laugh at such statements. But in the late 1970s and early 1980s, some prophecy teachers were looking at the new coin as a possible sign of the end. Many proclaimed the collapse of the dollar and the birth of a new money system that would eventually force a new world financial order controlled by a supercomputer. Although prophecy teachers avoid discussing the Anthony coin these days, themes of a new money system and persistent rumors that a giant computer called "the Beast," located in Brussels, Belgium, that's poised to take over the world's banking system, are rampant and widely believed.

For that we can thank prophecy teachers like Deal. In 1979 he also helped popularize the alleged computer. Quoting an "expert" source in his book, Deal claimed the computer was created to pull the world together in the event of "world chaos. . . . Common Market leaders during a crisis meeting in Brussels, Belgium, were introduced to the 'Beast,' a gigantic computer that occupies three floors of the Administration Building at the Common Market Headquarters. The computer is capable of assigning a number to every person on earth in the form of a laser tattoo. Then, through infrared scanners, this invisible tattoo would appear on a screen."[3]

The Southwest Radio Church was on to the story of the "Beast of Brussels" four years earlier. In 1966 they reported that a computerized, cashless society was coming, and in 1975 Southwest reported that the computer "Beast" was being constructed that "would connect banks in Canada, the Common Market, and the USA." An article in Southwest's 1977 newsletter discussing the beast computer said, "What we are projecting here is a socialistic economic leveling and a new money system in the 1980s."[4]

In another Southwest booklet, published in 1979, Patrick

Fisher, a computer expert from Canada, said that the Beast of Brussels was already tracking "every move" of individuals from "almost all of the trading nations" into the memory banks, which would eventually result in all credit cards being eliminated in favor of a new credit card that "everyone must have":

> It [the Beast] has been in existence for four years or so. Through use of credit cards, it has been easy to put almost all the trading nations into the memory banks. . . . Every move you have made, and every penny that you have paid to Internal Revenue each year is all on record. The computer capacity was set for 2 billion people four years ago. Every individual, along with every move he has made, any change of address, information concerning his job and his earning capacity, has been recorded.[5]

Does This Beast Exist?

Despite the frightening statements of our tracking and eventual control by a European computer, these reports—and others of a planned new money system—are greatly exaggerated. The soothsayers have quoted no top-notch international economists—or even a local college professor well versed in international finances—to back up their claims. Fisher's claim that all IRS records are in a European computer is based on total hearsay. On the basis of existing privacy laws, it is illegal for the IRS to release any personal or tax information to anyone—or anything—for *any reason.*

During a recent visit to the Internal Revenue Service's massive regional computer center, which covers most of the Middle Atlantic states and Puerto Rico, I discovered there are strict security measures—measures even locked into the computer software—that make it extremely difficult for taxpayer information to get out to individual IRS employees. The massive computer room, in the bowels of a federal building in Philadelphia, is under strict twenty-four-hour guard.

The soothsayers who make wild claims about computers and the alleged new money system apparently have not checked with any informed economists in an attempt to see if they were true. Had they done so, they would have found out that the "Beast" exists only in their fertile imaginations.

As a result of this eagerness to believe many wild rumors, the rumors themselves have taken on a life of their own and have been blown out of proportion. To some, the mythical computer has taken on demonic characteristics, as it is perceived as being at the center of a massive conspiracy, orchestrating mankind's enslavement and ruin. Consider the statements found in a circa 1979 issue of the *Awakeners Newsletter* of North Jersey:

> It has been written in the Biblical Book of Revelations [sic] what is beginning to happen in today's world, that a vast conspiracy by certain banking interests in the U.S. and abroad are deliberately wrecking the economy of the U.S. and planning a world-wide depression that will make the Great Depression of the 30's pale in comparison. . . . [there will be a stock market crash in] October of 1979 [that] will begin the Tribulation [and] will culminate in this laser "Mark of the Beast" . . . The European Common Market Computer at Brussels, Belgium . . . [is] . . . pre-fixed by the numbers 666. It is called the Beast by those who built it and work on it. . . . The Beast has many tentacles in the Mafia, the CIA, the Knights of Malta and other sinister organizations which have been working for many years together to bring this enslavement about. Those who accept the "Mark of the Beast" will spend time in Hades after passing over in death. This alone is worth thinking about. In January of 1979 we were told that the current Pope in Rome is an actor, a look-alike for the real Pope who was murdered in this World-Wide conspiracy. Also recently President Carter was injected with cancer [leukemia] by agents of the Beast who need him replaced by one more obedient in this world-wide plan to enslave humanity.[6]

Dr. James McKeever of Medford, Oregon, both teaches prophecy and is a renowned economist. His *McKeever Strategy* letter has consistently been well regarded in the field of finance. McKeever, who has even installed large computer systems, almost winces when he hears such talk about a computer takeover. He wrote:

> People are concerned about the "3-story computer in Brussels that is called the beast that is capable of numbering every human being on the earth." The computer in Brussels is the SWIFT computer. SWIFT stands for System for Worldwide Individual Financial Transactions. It functions primarily as a clearing house computer between banks but can also be used for individual financial transactions.
>
> I have talked to one of the key men who installed the system and it is not three stories high and is located deep in the basement of a building there in Brussels.
>
> . . . As far as the SWIFT system in Brussels being called "the beast," I've installed many, many computer systems and there is rarely one that somebody doesn't call "the beast," "the monster" or something even less complimentary when he is having difficulties debugging it and shaking down the system.[7]

McKeever said the computer is not engineering the takeover of the world, and it is not gathering information on or even tracking individuals throughout the free world.

Is the Beast in Our Money?

Closely related to this mythical beast are rumors of a new money system. One frightening rumor still circulating is that the United States government had accidentally issued checks requiring a mark in the forehead or hand in order to cash them. In fact, California prophecy teacher Charles Taylor has been issuing a 666 tract that states:

> Scores of Social Security checks were accidentally mailed to recipients that required a special and un-

> usual process for cashing. It was so unusual that banks refused to even try to cash them. The instructional paragraph of these particular checks was changed to read that the party cashing the check MUST HAVE THE PROPER IDENTIFICATION MARK IN THEIR RIGHT HAND OR FOREHEAD. Without it, the check could not be cashed. . . . These government checks, requiring a MARK in a person's RIGHT HAND OR FOREHEAD are not to be put into use UNTIL NEEDED.

Taylor further claimed in the tract, "From Florida to Washington to California I have reports of almost 100 persons who received the 'forehead or hand' Social Security checks. My own bills now have on them either 66, 99, or 666. The technology is here. Bible prophecy is ready for fulfillment. The time is at hand!"[8]

But when later questioned about the alleged government checks, Taylor said: "I haven't seen an actual check, no. I have talked to people in the realm of rumor. I've talked to people about it, but I haven't actually seen one."

How can we be sure such checks were ever issued, especially when the Social Security Administration has labeled the rumors as false?

"I don't think there can be that much smoke without there being some fire," Taylor said. "But I don't have any verifiable [evidence], I don't have a photograph of one [a check] or anything like that."

Why does Taylor still issue the tract, treating it as fact, when he can't prove it exists? (In an early version of the tract, Taylor listed the address of a Chattanooga, Tennessee, ministry that allegedly had proof of the hand and forehead government checks. But now Taylor says he doesn't know how to locate the ministry. Directory assistance operators in Tennessee say no such ministry is listed in that area code.)

"The main thing is the salvation message that's on it," he said, explaining why he's still issuing the tract. "Know the

Lord and you won't have to worry about the mark of the beast. That's the intent and purpose of it."[9]

New Money Coming?

What about those rumors that the United States government is going to soon begin calling in all the greenback dollars and replacing them with new money? In a February 5, 1984, seminar, prophecy teacher Doug Clark claimed the new money, which he referred to as "rainbow" or "technicolor money" was already printed and set to go out before March, 1985. Clark added that it would take about ten months to change over to the new money, and that would lead to a depression. There would be no check writing by the end of the eighties. Possibly "by 1985 or by 1987–1988," a cashless system would be in place where computers would do all the banking.[10] Obviously, none of that has happened.

Does Dr. James McKeever think there's a new money system coming? What does he think of a shift to it?

First of all, he said, there's nothing to fear from the United States government printing new money. It's been done "at least thirty times since we've been a nation," he said. "I think that's one fear that teachers keep playing off of that's absolutely ridiculous.

"Some of the old dollar bills I have in my collection you would be amazed at. People look at them and ask, 'Is that U.S. currency?' Indeed they are dollar bills. They are going to change the dollar bill once again, which will be no big thing," he said.

McKeever explained that the government's motive in a possible shift to a new dollar someday has nothing to do with the Antichrist. It has more to do with counterfeiters. "The problem is there are color copiers now that can copy a dollar bill well enough that you can put the copy in a dollar bill money changer and get out coins. In fact, if you go out and buy 100 percent rag linen paper at any stationery store, they will have to take down your name and address" because of the government's concern.

"I printed a photo in the *End-Times News Digest* [his ministry's publication] of what the new money was going to look like. It's going to have 'United States' written multiple times, too small for a copier to pick up, around the picture, and it will also have a vertical bar across the middle of the left-hand side." He said that since a changeover would be a one-to-one exchange of the old money with the new, there's little chance the move would result in a depression or anything ominous. The exchange must be made on a one-to-one basis, he said, or else every computer program in the world that calculates based on the United States dollar, such as all payroll, inventory, and reservation systems, would have to be changed simultaneously. Forget any ten-to-one or one-hundred-to-one rumors. That will not happen, McKeever flatly states.

McKeever explained that about three years ago Japan came out with a new currency, and prophecy teachers were declaring that it was part of a steady march toward the Antichrist's economic system. But the truth of the matter was that "it was just a giant non-event, so they [the prophecy teachers] went on to the next thing that looked scary."

He emphasized that there may be a time in the future when we should be concerned about a new money system, but not now. Not until a new economic system requires someone to take a mark or pledge allegiance to or worship an individual.

> I'm sixty and when they first came out with the checks with the funny-looking characters across the bottom—magnetic incoded character recognition (MICR)—many Christians said that this was part of the mark of the beast and were concerned that the government would be able to track everything they spent. Now nobody thinks anything about using those. Then credit cards came out, and that was a big bugaboo, and now debit cards are coming out, and that's the big bad guy. If Christ tarries, a hundred years from now we might be making financial transactions

> with little plastic discs or something or with our thumbprints.
>
> As long as an economic system does not require you to worship the beast, it's not part of the beast system. So people should stop worrying.[11]

Not only has no one asked us to worship a human recently, no one has been *forced* to take the numbers people have clamored about. Therefore none of these candidates for the mark of the beast have fulfilled the prophetic statement of Revelation 13:16.

What Kind of Beast Would Do This?

As people try to turn the beast of Revelation 13:11–18 into a computer, we need to take a look at the nature of the Antichrist and what he will be able to do.

- He is described as a leader who will seize the kingdom through intrigue (Daniel 11:21).
- He will sit with another king at the same table (Daniel 11:27).
- He is called "the man of lawlessness. . . , the man doomed to destruction" (2 Thessalonians 2:3).
- He will have power to do miraculous signs, causing fire to come from heaven (Revelation 13:13).
- He will have power to give breath to the first beast (Revelation 13:15).
- He will be captured and cast into the lake of fire (Revelation 19:20).

There seems to be a rather human element to the actions in which the beast takes part. After all can you imagine a computer going into the lake of fire?

Though mankind may use computers or other machines to do the evil that will be part of the very end days, the people behind the machines will take the blame—and the judgment of God. If we're going to look for a beast, let's look where Scripture points.

8
666 Madness

To many of us who remember that day in 1981, the scene kept playing itself over and over again in our minds. The television networks didn't help much, either, by replaying the scene over and over again.

President Ronald Reagan stepped out of a Washington, D. C., hotel when suddenly, *bang! bang! bang! bang! bang!* in spitfire motion, the shots rang out. Within seconds, Secret Service agents were all over John Hinckley, who had shot the president to "prove" his love for a Hollywood actress.

Fortunately, Reagan's life was spared, and before long he was back to work. But gravely injured—shot in the head at point-blank range—was Reagan's press secretary, James Brady. At first, everyone thought Brady had been killed. CBS's Dan Rather even had a moment of silence for him while on the air that confusing day.

In those days some overzealous Christians started a quiet rumor. Could Ronald Wilson Reagan, whose first, middle and last names each contain six characters—666—be the Antichrist? Could the near-death of Brady—one of the heads of Reagan's government—be a prophetic sign? After all, Revelation 13:3 says: "One of the heads of the beast seemed to have had a fatal wound, but the fatal wound had been healed. The whole world was astonished and followed the beast."

Of course the rumor was silly. And many—quite rightly—thought it was ridiculous right off the bat and said so. One can construe the numbers 666 out of almost anything—even anyone's name—with enough effort. That doesn't mean it has anything to do with the Antichrist, and many prophecy teachers ought to know better than to search for the number *666* underneath every rock.

Take Mary Stewart Relfe's best-selling book *When Your Money Fails,* for example. In its pages Relfe reads the number of the beast into the most unlikely places. By doing so, she has libeled many, implying they are working together in a gigantic conspiracy to usher in the Antichrist. As mentioned earlier, an unfortunate libel was leveled at the late Anwar Sadat, whom she compared with Adolf Hitler.[1]

It is comforting to know that Relfe did issue a small disclaimer of sorts on the copyright page: "Information in this book is not an indictment against any product, person, or institution, financial or otherwise. . . ." But it's not very comforting—especially for young Christians trying to separate fact from fiction about the end times—to look at the disclaimer in her best-selling (and equally controversial) 1982 sequel, *The New Money System.* It states, more or less, that you can't trust Relfe's facts: "The Publisher endeavors to print only information from sources believed reliable, but absolute accuracy cannot be guaranteed."[2]

The thesis of the book is simple: The 666 system of the Antichrist is already here, and we're unwittingly using it in many forms, the chief of which is the supermarket bar codes now stamped on most products. To prove her point, Relfe claims that the digits *666* are cropping up everywhere.

For example, during the decade of the sixties, we might have been able to discern Bible prophecy from the Apollo space program. These were just some of the signs from an Apollo mission the discerning might have been able to see, wrote Relfe, who was quoting another author:

- "Apollo" has "6" letters.
- Each of the astronaut's names has six letters: *Lovell, Anders,* and *Borman*—"666." [By the way, why weren't the astro-

nauts on the first lunar launch mentioned? Is it because their names—Armstrong, Aldrin, and Collins—do not have six digits each?]

- From space, "6" television transmissions were made.
- The moon trip was a "6" day journey.
- The spacecraft was in "6" sections.
- The astronauts' section plus the escape system was "66" feet tall.
- This Apollo flight grossed out at "6" million pounds.
- To escape earth's gravity, it had to achieve a velocity of "6" miles per second.
- Enroute [sic] time to the moon was "66" hours.[3]

Or take some signs from the nation of Israel, she wrote. Some Israeli lottery tickets have on them the digits *666*. (The lottery was simply a game similar to many pick-six or -seven lottery games we have in the United States.[4] Some Israeli license plates have the number *666* on them.[5] Even more ominous, the late Egyptian President Anwar Sadat, who later made peace with Israel, was once the passenger on a warship on the Suez that happened to have the number *666* on its bow.[6]

From there, Relfe goes on to list dozens of products, bank statements, government documents, credit cards, and anything else she could conceive of that contained the numbers *666*. She even pulled a United States government symbol into the book, and implies that it could be the mark of the beast. Notice the horizontal *666* on a United States government logo:[7]

To Relfe, it doesn't matter if there is only one six in her dizzying illustrations of people's credit cards, shirt labels, and various serial numbers. The important thing is that it may be part of the Antichrist system. In someone's VISA-card payment coupon that she prominently displayed, she highlighted the fact that it had the number "699" on it. No matter, she wrote, "the sixes are programmed inverted . . . it is still '666.' "[8] (Would Relfe prefer to eliminate the numbers six and nine from our numeric system in the same way some hotel buildings skip the thirteenth floor?)

When displaying another person's MasterCard statement that happened to have the number *66* on it, Relfe wrote ominously that "in August 1980, MasterCharge began their switchover to MasterCard which bears the number '66.' "[9] This is not true.

The folks at VISA took another beating from Relfe when she used strange logic to claim that it stands for the mark of the beast. She wrote: "VISA is 6 6 6; Vi, *Roman* Numeral, is 6; the 'zz' sound, Zeta, the 6th character in the *Greek* alphabet, is 6; a, *English* is 6 [implying that the letter *a* turned backwards is a 6]."[10]

Such reasoning is not worthy of further comment. Are we supposed to avoid the numbers *six* and *nine* because of the possibility they have something to do with Antichrist? The answer is obvious: There's nothing wrong with six or nine or even three random six digits in a row.

Yet many Christians have jumped on the 666 bandwagon. Relfe's book—and many others out there like it—has done a disservice to the church. How many pastors have had to quell rumors about the Antichrist system because of Relfe's book, which sold more than 666,000 copies?

Let's hear some words of wisdom from James McKeever, who has dealt with many similar rumors in the past:

> There is currently much being written and said about the "666 system" and the mark of the beast. This has created a great deal of concern in the body of Christ. Since I am an economist, as I travel around to speak to Christian groups, people ask me if the VISA or MasterCharge cards are part of the mark of the beast

> and if they should destroy them. They are concerned that they may be accidentally taking on the mark of the beast. Other Christians are concerned that they will not be strong enough to resist receiving the mark of the beast. Many of these Christians are experiencing fear in various degrees. Unfortunately that fear is totally unfounded, as far as I'm concerned, and does not come from God.
>
> There is so much misinformation being put forth from well-meaning Christian broadcasters and authors that it would require several books to set the record straight. All I can hope to do . . . [is] to try to help . . . [people] . . . get rid of any fear that they may have and let God replace it with His peace.[11]

When we are wallowing in—or delighting in—fear, we do not use the gifts God has given us in His service. "For God hath not given us the spirit of fear; but of power, and of love, and of a sound mind." Paul goes on to admonish Timothy, "Be not thou therefore ashamed of the testimony of our Lord . . ." (2 Timothy 1:7, 8 KJV).

Do our lives testify to Christ—or do they testify to fear?

9
The Birds and the Bees and Other Horrors

The grade-B horror movie *The Swarm*, released in 1978, was about clouds of killer bees attacking and killing thousands of people in scenes reminiscent of Alfred Hitchcock's classic *The Birds*.

The film was apparently inspired by news reports of swarms of a new kind of bee heading north from South America to the Texas border. It all began around 1957, when twenty-six wild African queen bees and some of their workers were accidentally released near Sao Paulo, Brazil, during a bee-breeding experiment. Their mating with the more docile European bees, found in the Western Hemisphere, resulted in superdefensive bees. These bees sometimes attack animals and people who merely wander too close to their hives.

In 1989, they were expected to reach the United States, after moving northward about 300 miles per year since the accident. But scientists weren't too worried about it, because one killer-bee sting is no more harmful than any other bee sting. At most, only four out of 1 million Americans face being killed by the bees each year, experts say.[1]

According to the *Philadelphia Inquirer*, "Although the researchers and other experts fear the bees' arrival, they say they are more worried about something potentially worse: a media-driven panic that could leave Americans with the attitude that all bees are about as trustworthy as pit bulls."[2] Already government officials in Texas are busy passing out pamphlets telling people not to panic, because there is little danger.

Despite the facts, some prophecy teachers have latched on to the "killer bee" scare and have attached demonic qualities to them and implied that they may be part of one of God's most frightening judgments against man.

"It is expected that these killer bees will reach the U.S. by the late 1980's," wrote Pennsylvania prophecy teacher Salem Kirban in 1977. "How interesting in light of the Fifth Trumpet judgment of the Tribulation Period when for 5 months people are subjected to the painful stings of a new strain of locusts. See Revelation 9:3–12."[3]

For starters, bees are *not* locusts. These so-called killer bees have no resemblance to the description found in Revelation 9:7–10:

> The locusts looked like horses prepared for battle. On their heads they wore something like crowns of gold, and their faces resembled human faces. Their hair was like women's hair, and their teeth were like lions' teeth. They had breastplates like breastplates of iron. . . . They had tails and stings like scorpions, and in their tails they had power to torment people for five months.

These locusts couldn't be insects, much less bees, by that definition! But tales of killer bees and other future menaces, real or imagined, do serve two purposes: They make speculating on the news more interesting—and more important, perhaps, to some ministries—they scare the willies out of people.

False Alarm or Scare Tactic?

Speaking of the bees, let's talk about the birds. A while ago some prophecy teachers circulated stories about a massive influx of vultures and buzzards into Israel—even a new breed of vultures. Presumably God had sent them to the plains of Megiddo to get ready for the feast of their lives. Their seven-month-long dinner? The Russian army, of course. Some of them are "already circling in the Valley of Armageddon," said one report, perhaps implying that they were there to feed upon all the armies of the world that were soon to gather there for the last battle.

In the October, 1980, issue of *Chosen People* magazine, Harold Sevener conducted an intensive investigation of the report and concluded the statements were "completely false. . . . Those who claim that the vultures are an indication of an impending Armageddon misunderstand what the Scriptures teach. Such rumors, based upon a misunderstanding of Scripture, can greatly mislead the child of God. We need to carefully divide the Word of God, and this becomes all the more important as we see the end of this age coming to a close."[4]

Even though the vulture story was spurious and some prophecy teachers knew they couldn't verify it, *they reported on it anyway.*[5] This raises an important question: Do some ministries deliberately try to instill fear into their supporters? It sure looks that way, and some longtime prophecy teachers mentioned in this book agree.

Comments Hart "Rapture Alert" Armstrong:

> All these wild stories being told around which are scaring people, are unfounded and ridiculous. I am convinced, in some cases, they are in the imaginations of preachers who are trying to excite people to read their books, to listen to their programs, and to send money to their cause.[6]

Dr. James McKeever, who's been involved in a longtime effort to examine the signs of the times, claims some prophecy ministries attract thrill seekers:

> The two things that sell are fear and greed. If you want to make money, write a book about how to get rich off the coming famine or some other disaster. You'll sell a ton of copies because you have both the fear and the greed. I think some ministries take advantage of the fact that people will pay money to get scared to death—like paying money to go on a roller coaster or to see a horror movie. Christians who don't go to movies and don't ride roller coasters possibly look at these teachers of prophecy to keep them scared to death. I hate to say it, but they get a thrill out of it, just as they would from the roller coaster.[7]

What are some of the other frightening "last days" rumors out there?

- That President Jimmy Carter signed legislation which "cancels the right of Americans to own private property."[8]
- That F and H symbols ("forehead" and "hand") were being placed on supermarket bar codes as a preliminary to the Antichrist's system. Relfe only suggested this,[9] but California prophecy teacher Charles Taylor presented it as fact in his "666" tract. When questioned about it, Taylor admitted that he was told random F and H markings don't stand for "forehead" and "hand," but he said he is still publishing the tract. "The fact remains that the technology is there in which they can do it," he explained.[10]
- That Curtis Sliwa's crime-fighting "Guardian Angels" volunteer group may really be the Antichrist's secret army, poised to take over America at his command. Constance Cumbey's book *The Hidden Dangers of the Rainbow* drew parallels between the Angels and Hitler's brownshirts.[11] From there it was picked up and embellished substantially by Taylor, who implied they'd kill "Christians and Jews" on command:

> . . . The very aggressive Guardian Angels have spread across this nation. Purporting to help the police, groups are patrolling the streets in many cities of the U.S. and Canada. They soon expect to exceed 100,000 in number. I offer this warning: Beware of them, for their training is reportedly similar to that of Hitler's Brown Shirts and it is said they are being positioned for the purpose of furthering the cause of the New Age Movement by slaying Christians and Jews when they get the signal from the Hierarchy. That signal may come sooner than you think! According to THE PLAN of the New Age Movement, they reportedly have a timetable whereby they hope to have their domination complete by the summer solstice of 1983![12]

- That "scientists" believed the sun was about to nova, claiming the Jupiter Effect of 1982 "would set off the atomic collapse of the sun." Such an event describes some of the goings on of the great tribulation, such as the sun becoming unusually bright and hot and then becoming dark, according to David Webber and Noah Hutchings of the Southwest Radio Church.[13] (However, no scientists were quoted in any of the Southwest references that I saw. In fact, real scientists call these reports balderdash!)
- That the 1986 move to a nine-digit United States zip code is "in preparation for the global society of antichrist."[14]
- That war and earthquakes are coming sooner than you think. In 1987 the Southwest Radio Church, quoting a science magazine, implied that there'd be a "major earthquake in California along the San Andreas fault" in 1988.[15]

During the same year Taylor, citing "many" (but unnamed) "intelligence experts," confirmed that the "Soviet Union is mobilizing a major military confrontation with the United States sometime in 1988." Then he added, "In this year just before the rapture, INVEST IN HEAVEN AND REAP DIVIDENDS FOR ETERNITY. YOU CAN'T TAKE IT WITH YOU!"[16]

Similarly, Edgar Whisenant in his *88 Reasons* predicted a

horrific war between the United States and Soviet Union by using his own extrabiblical interpretation of Deuteronomy 28 that he claims applies exclusively to the United States. A war is coming "before the election in November 1988" that will leave only "about 200,000 people or less" alive out of America's "240 million," he wrote.[17]

During a recent appearance on TBN's "Praise the Lord" program, Doug Clark predicted World War III would begin within the next three years with the Russian invasion of Israel, as prophesied in Ezekiel 38. When asked by host Paul Crouch if the tribulation period will occur before the year 2000, Clark responded, "You bet!"[18] (When the United States bombed Libya, under the Reagan administration, Clark saw *that* as a sign that God would put hooks in the jaws of the Russians. Many viewers held their breaths until that crisis passed.)

Of course, the threat of imminent war has always been used by some prophecy teachers. In the late 1970s and early 1980s, many were crying to "rearm America" to ward off a perceived Russian military edge. In his *Survival Letter* of May 7, 1981, Doug Clark claimed the newly created United States Rapid Deployment Forces meant that "war is definitely anticipated by our leaders in the very foreseeable future."

Fiber-Optics Fears

One of the most astoundingly creative—and ridiculous—fear-mongering devices yet discovered by soothsayers is the idea that the Antichrist may be watching you right now through your television set. (So if you have a TV in the room, go cover it up before you read further!) The method may be through fiber optics, a relatively new electrical innovation that sends electronic digital light signals through miniature glass fibers instead of the traditional wires that feed into your cable outlet to your television set.

Remarked Emil Gaverluk and Patrick Fisher in Southwest's 1979 book, *Fiber Optics: The Eye of the Antichrist:*

> There is a pinhead-sized camera lens on the end of the fiber optic which can watch anything taking place in the room, including the reactions of the viewers to any specific program. This data is recorded on computers which can collate all remarks pro or con, to implement dictatorial control by any group or individual. The startling thing is that this fish-eye camera lens can still see and record everything, EVEN WHEN THE TELEVISION SET IS NOT TURNED ON. This means that every family will be under 24-hour surveillance. What a perfect setup for the Antichrist![19]

Later in the same book Fisher claimed that computers working in conjunction with "the Beast" computer in Brussels, had "already dropped the flag that says, 'Go now.' " to begin a major mid-East or possibly world war![20]

Ask any expert in electronics about Gaverluk and Fisher's fiber-optics theory, as I did, and you'll most likely get a hearty laugh. In the first place, the theory never addresses the fact that even if it is true that one can see through fiber-optics strands (and it's not, since they are only designed for digital electronic signals), the book never mentions that the optic lines are plugged in to a metal outlet plug or metal jack in a phone, which nothing can see past. (So it's all right now to uncover your television set and read on.)

Despite the absurdity of the theory, the fiber-optics scare has swept certain Christian circles. Relfe, for example, talked about it prominently in her book *When Your Money Fails.*[21]

Visions of the Future

A possible invasion of killer bees isn't the only reason we should fear our future, according to Salem Kirban. As probably the most prolific writer of all of today's prophecy teachers, Kirban has given us plenty of reasons to fear the future.

In 1970 Kirban came out with his book *I Predict.* It was a detailed look at what he thought the future held for the world, and obviously Kirban was expecting the tribulation soon. Kirban, however, was careful to say the book was only his opinion. On page 2 he stated: "My predictions are *NOT* given as occult phenomena, crystal ball reading or astrology. These are condemned by the Bible. . . . *Mine are based on human judgment and may or may not come true.*"

Here's some of the frightening things Kirban foresaw:

> In 1975 droughts will curtail farm production. Americans will come face to face with the fact that food is scarce!
>
> By 1982 special breathing masks will be common, starting first in Japan. Los Angeles will witness thousands of deaths caused by pollutants.
>
> By 1983 several cities will have trees in museums because of their scarcity.
>
> Spy lamposts will be installed in many areas by 1977. . . .
>
> By 1983 it will be necessary for the Capital of the U.S. to move from Washington.
>
> By 1980 the U.S. Government will be on the verge of collapse. By 1978 many in the U.S. will openly campaign for a dictator-type President.
>
> Before 1985 New York City will experience both a devastating hurricane and catastrophic earthquake.
>
> A head transplant will be undertaken in 1978.
>
> By 1980 conditions in the world and particularly the United States will reach riot proportions. The nation's water supply will be infused with a drug to calm the populace. Before 1980 the United States will resort to a dictatorial-type government.
>
> . . . In the 1980's church property will be confiscated.
>
> Within the next 15 years I predict the United States will merge with European nations under one dictatorial-type leader.
>
> . . . Full control of the news media will occur before 1982. The excuse given by the government will be that control is being instituted to "avoid internal chaos and achieve national security."
>
> I predict a U.S. war with China within the next 15 years.[22]

The record shows that an overwhelming number of Kirban's predictions *did not* come true. A few of them did. But since Kirban never claimed to be a prophet, that's not the point. The question is is it all right to scare people into the kingdom by unwarranted fear?

That's what Kirban tried to do with this book—and I suspect with many other of his books. Kirban has written more than fifty books, the vast majority of them on Bible prophecy. As he wrote in *I Predict*'s foreword, called "Why I Wrote This Book": "For out of this holocaust of horror . . . there is a way out for you, personally!" (If one receives Christ as personal Saviour.)

I believe in Kirban's salvation message. It is the same as mine.

He also deserves credit for being quick to take issue with Whisenant's *88 Reasons* on the basis it is unscriptural. Some of Kirban's books in the 1970s made a definite impression on my life.

But many of his writings have oversensationalized the news, and I cannot agree with that. The present condition of the world is ominous enough without making up more ways—often inaccurate ones—to make it more scary. Don't the Scriptures already say that in the time of the end, "Men's hearts shall fail them for fear"? (*See* Luke 21:26).

Just recently I awoke in the middle of the night in a cold sweat. I was having a nightmare that an atomic missile had been fired on Philadelphia, our hometown, and my wife and I were trying to flee.

It wasn't an unusual dream. Since the advent of the nuclear age many people today feel frightened. In these perilous times, thoughts like *what if it does happen?* are never that far below the surface of many minds. Come to think of it, there is probably a handful of missiles aimed at our city—and your city—right now. But concentrating on undue fear is counterproductive to the spread of the gospel.

What does Kirban say about his work today?

> I wrote [*I PREDICT*] . . . to show readers how current events can develop trends that eventually will usher in the end times. . . . Many [predictions] came true. Many did not. . . . In my research I look at news items not simply as news items but as *trends* that *eventually* will find their fulfillment in the Rapture and Tribulation Period. Each day brings us one day closer to this fulfillment.

I do wholeheartedly agree with his analysis of the church as we near the year 2000. In a March 28, 1988, statement for this book Kirban wrote that we're seeing the *greatest sign* of the end right now, yet the church is barely aware of it:

> In the last few years I have spoken in over 300 churches. I have noted a greater increase in Christian materialism and country-club Christianity. To me, this is the greatest sign of the end times. Psychology programs, money seminars, prosperity preaching have given us the gospel of self-esteem. It is time we get back to basics and back to Calvary . . . caring more about the lost souls who have not heard the Gospel of eternal redemption.[23]

Amen!

Part III
One Part Truth, Four Parts Fancy

I have to admire the soothsayers for one thing: They all seem to have vivid imaginations.

Of course they would deny their speculations are based on imagination. They would say they are based on Scripture or on some expert's opinion, no matter how fanciful that speculation might be.

Sometimes they build elaborate fantasies upon a small grain of biblical truth, and because there is a grain of truth, young Christians especially are often deluded.

God does not call us to believe every fancy that preachers or writers—even well-meaning ones—would have us accept. Instead he commands, "Do your best to present yourself to God as one approved, a workman who does not need to be ashamed and who correctly handles the word of truth" (2 Timothy 2:15).

Let us be certain our work holds to the truth of God's Word. Then none of us will need to hang our heads in shame—now or on the last day.

10
The 6,000-Year Legend

Archbishop Ussher of Armagh, Ireland, was a very serious man. He spent years in the mid-seventeenth century studying Bible chronologies, trying to fix dates on specific events. In 1654 Ussher announced his results to the world: Creation had taken place on October 26, 4004 B.C., at nine o'clock in the morning. Because of his status as a respected theologian, Ussher's chronology gained acceptance. An unknown authority even inserted it as a marginal reference in the King James Version of the Bible.[1]

Today, however, few Bible scholars take Ussher's date seriously. Even conservative scholars who are reluctant to accept a scientific dating of creation of billions of years ago do not want to be identified with Archbishop Ussher. Not only was Ussher unaware of geology, he also seems to have been unaware of biblical Hebrew.

Despite Ussher's chronology being debunked as unscholarly decades ago, today's end-times soothsayers still rely on it to "prove" a pet theory many of them hold in common. The theory I call the "6,000-year-human-history error" is used by almost all of today's date setters and prophecy sensationalists.

The theory goes something like this: Since the Scriptures

speak of six days of work and the seventh as the sabbath, and 2 Peter 3:8 says that a day with the Lord is like 1,000 years, then 6,000 years of human history will mark the end of the present age. The seventh day will mark the day of rest, or a 1,000-year millennial day of peace. Many soothsayers rely upon Ussher's 4004 B.C. date and add 6,000 years to it to come up with the end of this age—October 26, 1996. Deducting seven years from that, to account for a seven-year tribulation, they arrive at a 1988 or 1989 date for the rapture of the church.

This type of thinking, with slight variations, in fact, made up Whisenant's reason 16 in his book *88 Reasons Why the Rapture Will Be in 1988*. One of the variations was that Whisenant was using *The Chronological Bible,* instead of Ussher's chronology. He began counting 6,000 years forward from "4005 B.C. . . . the year that Adam would have been born." He concluded reason 16 by stating: "The 6,000 years or the six days with God appears to end or be complete in the year 1995, allowing for 1988 to be the time that the 70th week of Daniel [a time some prophecy teachers believe refers to the tribulation] would begin."[2]

What's wrong with the 6,000-year theory? Right off, a close and complete reading of 2 Peter 3:8 gives us an answer, according to Ralph Woodrow in his book, *His Truth Is Marching On: Advanced Studies on Prophecy in the Light of History:*

> The Bible says that "one day is with the Lord as a thousand years," but it also says "and a thousand years as one day" (2 Peter 3:8). This could not prove that a day equals a thousand years, any more than it could prove that a thousand years equals a day. It simply shows that God is not limited by our ideas of time.[3]

Woodrow added that the 6,000-year teaching "appeared for the first time in the ancient book called 'Secrets of Enoch' (chapter 32). Later it was referred to in the 'Epistle of

Barnabas.' "[4] Both books, despite their rejection as part of the canon centuries ago, are heavily relied upon by today's date setters.

Let's look at some of the variations of the 6,000-year theory by today's teachers.

R. Henry Hall in *AD 1991—The Genesis of Holocaust* says:

> From the First coming of Christ to the Day of the Lord is also a period of 2,000 years, or, the final "6" in the trilogy of the plan of GOD. Three distinct periods of 2,000 years will be fulfilled literally in 1998 and still man has not learned from history. . . . We know now that GOD is going to PROTECT the born-again believer from His wrath against the non-believer and we have learned that He has allowed mankind 6,000 years to repent of his transgressions.[5]

Reginald E. Dunlop uses what he called an exclusive interpretation of Exodus 23:10, supplied to him by the "Holy Spirit," to affirm the 6,000-year theory:

> His Plan included six-thousand years in which man could obey His covenants and find His infinite blessing, OR, choose to disobey His commandments and find themselves on the outside of His eternal reward. . . . In Exodus 23:10, GOD gives us another clue as to the destiny of mankind.
>
> "And SIX YEARS (6,000) thou shalt sow thy land (labor), and shalt gather in the fruits thereof (living on earth in the dominion of satan):
>
> "But the SEVENTH YEAR thou shalt let it rest."[6]

Hart Armstrong asserts:

> We know the Bible records approximately 2,000 years from Adam to Abraham, and 2,000 years from Abraham to Christ. As we approach the end of the final 2,000 years (six thousand years in all), we can well

> expect God to end His labors, and to bring to Earth His King, the Messiah, the Lord Jesus Christ. . . . This means that our calendar is actually four years behind God's calendar. So the year in which we are now living (1988) is actually 1992 according to God's calculation. Thus we can see that God's Calendar will reach the year 2,000 by 1996. . . . If the Tribulation period is to take place before, and will be completed at the Battle of Armageddon . . . subtracting seven years from 1996 brings us back to 1989. If the time for the possible beginning of the Tribulation period may occur as early as 1989, (by our "supposings") then what can we look for to occur in 1989?[7]

Post-tribulation-rapture prophecy teacher James McKeever has also affirmed the 6,000-year theory in his *End Times News Digest*. But McKeever wrote that the 6,000-year period "could end sometime between now and the year 2030," if the final 2,000 years of human history began with Christ's resurrection in A.D. 29 "or, more likely, between now and 1996."[8]

Colin Deal's controversial 1979 book, *Christ Returns by 1988: 101 Reasons Why*, solidly confirms his belief in the 6,000-year theory, and he uses it as a proof that the rapture could take place in 1988 or before.[9] When 1988 came and went without the rapture occurring, Deal backpedaled in a March 17–18, 1989, radio interview and used the same 6,000-year theory to strongly imply a rapture in the early 1990s. In the Southwest Radio Church interview, he didn't explain what went wrong with his earlier rapture date.

J. R. Church, author of the 1986 book *Hidden Prophecies in the Psalms* (the hypothesis being that the number of each Psalm correlates to the 1900s; that is, Psalm 48 is 1948, and so on), also proposes a 1988 rapture date using the 6,000-year theory. He declared, "The Son of God will soon appear to establish a heavenly throne on earth. The next thousand years will be paradise!"[10] Church claims Psalm 90:4, "For a thousand years in your sight are like a day that has just gone by, or like a watch in the night," confirms the 6,000-year theory, when the verse merely states that a thousand years in God's sight is like yesterday.

Church incorrectly claims that Psalm 90:10 sets the time period for "the last generation . . . somewhere between seventy and eighty years, and those years after seventy will be filled with labor and sorrow. Perhaps those are the years of tribulation."[11] But the passage does not refer to the last generation, as Church claims; it clearly alludes to the *life expectancy of man* and the struggles of life: "The length of our days is seventy years—or eighty if we have the strength; yet their span is but trouble and sorrow. . . ."

David Webber and Noah Hutchings not only teach the 6,000-year theory and cite Ussher's chronology;[12] Webber also uses numerology and speculations drawn from the Great Pyramid of Giza in Egypt to prove it!

> The creative number of the world is six. "For in six days the Lord made heaven and earth . . ." (Exodus 20:11). The number six is stamped upon the Great Pyramid which shows the juxtaposition of the earth relative to other planets in this solar system, and a time-table for earth history in multiples of six! There are also six dispensations of time in which God tested man upon the earth (Innocence, Conscience, Human Government, Promise, Law and Grace).[13]

Relfe also calls upon Ussher's research to "prove" the timing of the return of Christ: "It doesn't take a genius to see that God has allotted man 6,000 years to do his work and the seventh thousand-year period will be God's Sabbath, the Millennium Reign of the Government of Christ . . . though much scholarly work has subsequently been done, [Ussher's] timetable remains virtually unchanged."[14]

That's where Relfe is wrong. Today *very few* if any people knowledgeable in the field of Bible chronology certify Ussher's date, including spokesmen from some of the most conservative ministries. In a recent interview with biblical literalist Ken Ham, director of the Institute for Creation Research (ICR), in El Cajon, California, he told me that although he considers Ussher's work "reasonably good . . . some of us believe the possibility exists for gaps to be in the chronology. The possibility exists that the age of the earth is 6,000 or 7,000 years." Ham added that ICR's official position is that "the formation of the earth and the age of man is at the maximum of 10,000 B.C. (about 12,000) years old."[15]

Then there is Harold Camping, president of Family Stations, Inc., of Oakland, California. Camping usually comes down on the side of conservative—even literal—Bible interpretation. But while answering a recent question on his "Open Forum" radio show, Camping openly challenged Ussher's work and stated he believes the earth is about 13,000 years old.

Scientists, of course, believe the age of man is much older. They claim to have found detailed cave paintings in Les Eyzies, France, that are about 14,000 years old, and they say these can be traced to the Cro-Magnon man, who first appeared about 35,000 years ago.[16]

We can't say for sure how long ago Adam walked with God in the Garden of Eden, but apparently it was not 4004 B.C. Ussher's chronology—upon which today's soothsayers base their 6,000-year theory—is flawed. Here's why:

First of all, despite what the soothsayers publish, Ussher's chronology wasn't always recognized as the definitive one. Before Ussher, Calvisius, a Lutheran, had made similar calculations, which were used over a long span of time. Martin Luther's own calculations were in line with Calvisius's. They concluded that the world was created at about 4064 B.C.[17] In other words, if we believe the 6,000-year theory and use these earlier chronologies, the world is already about a half a century past the 6,000-year mark (and by the soothsayers' calculations well into the millennium)!

According to Paul A. Zimmerman's book of selective writings, *Rock Strata and the Biblical Record,* Ussher arrived at his calculations primarily by using genealogical tables in the

Scriptures, particularly in Genesis 5 and 11. But when we compare these genealogies with others in the Bible, we find evidence of generations being omitted. For example Matthew omits generations at two points, and the genealogies of 1 Chronicles 23:15, 16; 26:24 list only three generations during a 400-year period.[18] Stated Fred Kramer, who examined Ussher's chronology in the book:

> It is evident that many generations have here been omitted, as appears to be customary in the genealogies of both the Old and of the New Testament. . . . We must assume that the writer of Genesis 5 and 11 may possibly have followed the same method.[19]

Kramer also noted that there may have been substantial gaps in the Genesis genealogies. According to Ussher, the Tower of Babel was built 102 years after the end of the flood. How could eight people have multiplied in a 102-year time period to undertake an awesome project like the tower of Babel?[20]

Kramer does offer a solution to the puzzle. Could it be that the biblical genealogies were never placed in God's Word for us to calculate the age of the earth and the birth of man? "The Scripture is there because of Christ (Luke 24:44), and was written aforetime for our learning (Rom. 15:4), to make us wise unto salvation through faith which is in Christ Jesus (2 Tim. 3:15)," he wrote.[21] He also added:

> The genealogies are there to enable the believer to know that Jesus, whom he accepts as his Lord and Savior, was actually, as was prophesied, the son of David, the son of Abraham. How many generations were omitted in drawing up these genealogies is of no importance for our real purpose, which is to testify to Christ and to the fulfillment of prophecy in Him. That many generations were omitted seems evident.[22]

Then how old is the earth? Bible scholars differ widely on the subject, some adding a few thousand years or "at most a few tens of thousands of additional years" to Ussher's figure. "On the other hand, there are others who believe that the periods of time in question may have been almost interminably long, running into hundreds of thousands, and perhaps even millions of years."[23]

Despite these observations, some soothsayers have turned to unbiblical means to hold on to the 6,000-year theory. Last year popular Saint Petersburg, Florida, prophecy teacher Ray Brubaker offered copies of "The Epistle of Barnabas" on his "God's News Behind the News" prophecy show. In a two-page introduction to the epistle, written by Brubaker, he trumpets the fact that it affirms the 6,000-year theory and asks, "HOW CLOSE ARE WE TO THE END OF 6,000 YEARS OF HISTORY?" Henry Kreysler, who advertises his prophecy tapes extensively in *Charisma & Christian Life* magazine, under the name of "Watchman in the Wilderness," also uses a page from the Epistle of Barnabas that refers to the 6,000-year history in teaching material he sends out with prophecy tapes.

Chapter 13:5 of the Epistle of Barnabas states: "For with him one day is a thousand years: as himself testifieth, saying, Behold this day shall be as a thousand years. Therefore, children, in six days, that is in six thousand years, shall all things be accomplished."

But Brubaker and Kreysler don't mention that the epistle also alleges that hyenas change sex every year and that weasels conceive with their mouths. The epistle also charges that Judaism sprang from the deceit of a bad angel. Little wonder, then, that this so-called Epistle of Barnabas was not accepted as part of the New Testament.

In recent days other prophecy teachers—most noticeably Grant R. Jeffrey, a Canadian who has become a rising star among prophecy teachers due to his new book, *Armageddon: Appointment with Destiny* (Toronto: Frontier Research Publications, 1988)—have argued that the early church "without exception" accepted the 6,000-year theory, and they expected Christ to come back near the year 2000.[24] But Jeffrey's assertion is simply not true.

If life as we know it continues past the year 2000, many preachers and writers will have egg on their faces. Such people will have learned a hard lesson—that it is pure folly to put God in a box by trying to limit Him to our human calculations.

11
The *National Enquirer* of Christianity

Are scientists trying to decode radio signals from heaven? That's what David Webber implied in his book *Satan's Kingdom and the Second Coming*.

It's fascinating stuff. Webber claims that for quite some time scientists have been receiving coded signals from outer space and that many are "convinced that they emanate from a superior source of intelligence in the Heavens." He quotes an article claiming that scientists have deciphered radio messages "clearly outlining the constellation of Bootes (the Big Dipper) in the northern sky." Another scientist is quoted as saying that the messages "could have been beamed to Earth thousands of years ago, and have since been waiting for us to gain sufficient knowledge. . . ."

Webber then interjects that the prophet Daniel was told that in the end times knowledge shall be increased. Citing Psalm 48 and Isaiah 14:13, he adds that the "Heavenly Jerusalem" and the throne of God are also located in the northern sky—in the same direction the radio signals are coming from. "Certainly, we are witnessing many strange signs from heaven in these last days," he wrote.[1]

Contact from beyond! What a find! Have we finally progressed far enough to have received radio transmissions from God Himself? Why haven't we heard of this incredible breakthrough before? The answer is you would have if you had been reading the *National Enquirer*. Because it was from that oft-maligned (and often sued) supermarket tabloid (page 26 in the March 18, 1973, edition) that Webber got the inspiration for his radio-signals-from-space story.

But that's nothing new. Webber extensively quoted the *National Enquirer* in his Southwest Radio Church booklet *A Satanic Trilogy: Pyramid Power*, to explain what pyramid power is.[2] The *Bible in the News*, Southwest's magazine, also cites the *National Enquirer* frequently. In one issue it referred to a Transcendental Meditation experiment that supposedly affected the minds of almost everyone living in Rhode Island![3]

You may be surprised that the Southwest Radio Church, one of the oldest radio ministries in the country, uses such a questionable source. But it's a matter of routine with Southwest, so much so that some of its publications are beginning to resemble the tabloids. The outrageous and incredible stories they print make the Southwest Radio Church the *National Enquirer* of Christianity, attracting an audience with inquiring minds.

Southwest publishes all the latest pop-science fads, along with the latest projected dates for the great tribulation, the Second Coming of Christ, and the latest speculation on the identity of the Antichrist and the false prophet of the book of Revelation. No matter how outlandish the theories are, Webber and Hutchings and others usually find a way to insert a salvation message, along with Scripture passages to back up their constant, strange speculations.

Speculation on prophecy is a tradition with the Southwest Radio Church, which often opens its broadcasts with the proclamation, "God is still on the throne, and prayer changes things!" Noah Hutchings said that when he joined the ministry, in 1951, its founder, the late Dr. Edward F. Webber (the father of David Webber) was being attacked for pointing out the similarities of Hitler to the Antichrist.

"Of course Hitler was a madman sent out to destroy the Jews," said Hutchings. "He made a covenant with the Pope and Mussolini . . . there were a lot of similarities. [But] what if Hitler were the Antichrist? He [Webber] would have been failing in his responsibilities had he not pointed out the similarities."[4]

Let's look at some more speculations from the Southwest Radio Church in recent years, from the location of heaven to other realms habitated only by space cadets.

Where Is Heaven?

Dr. Emil Gaverluk, an author and longtime associate of Southwest, continues the theme that heaven is in the northern sky, as developed by Webber a decade earlier. He claims NASA may have charted it "using data obtained from high-flying" U-2 aircraft. It could be in the direction of Virgo, which is over 55 million light-years from us, he writes in his 1986 Southwest book, *The Rapture in the Old Testament*.

Gaverluk, reprinting an anonymous article, reports that NASA found a "supercluster" that may contain "a large-scale structure in the direction of Virgo." Does this pose a logistical problem for angels traveling that great a distance to the earth? No, suggests Gaverluk, quoting an official from the Institute for Creation Research, "THEY CAN FLY THROUGH SPACE AT INCREDIBLE SPEEDS, BILLIONS OF TIMES FASTER THAN EVEN THE SPEED OF LIGHT (Daniel 9:21–23)."[5]

Note that the proof text in Daniel reports only that the angel Gabriel came to the prophet in "swift flight." It says nothing about the famed angel flying through space at a clip even Superman couldn't begin to match. The interpretation of Isaiah 14:13 and Psalm 48, which Gaverluk and others quote to find the location of heaven, is sheer and unwarranted speculation.

The New Jerusalem Found?

Newsweek reported on a strange object in the sky, called SS 433, about 10,000 light-years away, that baffled scientists. According to the 1979 magazine article, the object was traveling at about 30,000 miles per second—and scientists had no idea what it was.

But Webber and Hutchings suggest this might be the New Jerusalem Revelation 21:2 (KJV) prophecies will come ". . . down from God out of heaven. . . ."[6]

Did Old Testament High Priests Communicate With God Via Laser Beams and Crystals?

Emil Gaverluk and Patrick Fisher proposed this idea in their fiber-optics book. They suggested that the priestly breastplate described in Exodus 28:30 may have been twelve jewels—"crystals"—representing the tribes of Israel. When the priest went into the Holy of Holies once a year to ask for forgiveness of sins, his breastplate may have been zapped with laser beams protruding from the "Shekinah glory" of God in a form of communication.

"Whether this communication was electronic or not, I do not know," said Fisher.

"I'm wondering if perhaps the light of God, His Shekinah glory, was shown in the form of a laser beam," Gaverluk responded. ". . . I talked to a surgeon about this, and he thought it could have been some kind of audio device. If this is true, it could have been a crystal. We're using crystals in our transistors."[7]

In their thinking it's only a coincidence that the crystals are frequently used in divination by New Agers.

Hell

Webber and Hutchings have definite ideas on where hell is. It could be in a white dwarf star, they suggest in a 1979 book. They jumped to that conclusion after they noted a New York University professor claimed that the white dwarf can never burn out. "IT IS ONLY TOO EVIDENT THAT THE LAKE OF FIRE HAS BEEN PREPARED AND IS NOW READY," they quoted the professor as saying.[8]

Or is hell in a black hole? ". . . a black hole [theorized by many scientists to be a collapsed star] can become a wormhole, also called an Einstein-Rosen bridge," noted Webber and Hutchings. "It is theorized that a space wormhole connects two universes, possibly where time is existent in one and anti-time in the other. Anyone trapped in a black hole within a wormhole would live forever in torment in a state of limbo. It is interesting to note that the biblical prophet spoke of the fate of the last in similar terminology: '. . . THEIR WORM SHALL NOT DIE, NEITHER SHALL THEIR FIRE BE QUENCHED . . .' (Isaiah 66:24)."[9]

Writing by himself, three years later, Hutchings cast another wild card into the hell-is-in-a-black-hole theory. He quoted a 1982 NASA report that suggested there may be a large object—perhaps a black hole—beyond the solar system, affecting the orbits of the farthest planets—Uranus, Neptune, and Pluto. Scientists have been looking for additional planets for a long time, due to the erratic orbits of these three. Hutchings then suggests that it could pull "our sun and all nine planets . . . into the black hole that is lurking just on the edge of outer space."[10]

Another possibility, according to some Southwest publications, is that Venus houses hell. Venus "is a literal bottomless pit, a hell hole burning with fire and brimstone. It is amazing that our own space agency had to resort to Bible terminology to report what is being discovered in outer space," wrote Webber and Hutchings.[11] On the other hand, they wrote, Venus, sometimes called the "morning star," will be inhabited by Christians someday! Didn't Jesus tell the church in Thyatira (Revelation 2:26–28) that if they overcame adversity he would give them the "morning star"? And isn't Venus known as the morning star?[12]

Did Job Refer to Life on the Moon?

Life on the moon may have been wiped out by an "astronomical catastrophe . . . possibly caused by the sun reaching a near nova stage," wrote Webber and Hutchings. Referring to Job 25:25, the two authors speculate that life might once have existed on the moon, but that the fall of Lucifer and the angelic rebellion caused this life to end.[13] Not only that, the cosmic conflict might have destroyed life on Mars.[14]

Other Space Tales

Webber and Hutchings also claim the Bible refers to "orbit windows," affirms that unidentified flying objects appeared at different times in the Old Testament, and describes travel in outer space. At times these "Christian" theories come close to sounding like Erich von Daniken's *Chariots of the Gods*, the pop-science book that sold millions of copies in the early 1970s and explained away the miracles of the Bible as being caused by the superior technology of space beings.

Webber and Hutchings reported that UFOs were used during a celestial invasion referred to in Genesis 6:2, when the " 'sons of God' (angels) left their created order (Jude 6) to live as men" and take wives. God also took Abram up in a UFO, which Genesis 15:12–18 describes as ". . . A SMOKING FURNACE, AND A BURNING LAMP. . . ," and showed him the boundaries of the land his descendants would inherit. A cloud of spaceships was also the pillar of cloud and pillar of fire that led the Israelites out of Egypt, and it was a spaceship that translated Elijah into heaven. Yes, the creature with wheels that Ezekiel reported seeing was a spaceship, according to Webber and Hutchings.[15]

Other prophecy teachers also have hinted that "clouds" referred to in the Bible could be flying saucers. Last year, on the weekly "God's News Behind the News" television show, host Ray Brubaker devoted a large portion of a program to the possibility that God will use flying saucers as the mode of transportation to catch the church up in the rapture.

Concerning man flying in outer space, Webber and

Hutchings tie it into the "last days" and eventually to the Antichrist himself:

> Does the Bible have anything to say about travel in outer space? missionary outreach from outer space? or beings who would come from outer space and intervene in the affairs of man? The answer to all these questions is a resounding "Yes!" These signs from heaven are warnings that the last generation should be prepared for the soon return of Jesus Christ, to come as Lord of lords and King of kings (Rev. 19:12–16).[16]

To back it up, the authors cite Deuteronomy 30:1–4. "If any of thine be driven out unto the outmost parts of heaven, from thence will the Lord thy God gather thee, and from thence will he fetch thee" (v. 4 KJV). The passage is used out of context, however. It actually prophesies the dispersion of the Jews throughout the world; it is not talking about space travel.

Webber and Hutchings conclude that God's Word said man would travel in space, and speculate that the Antichrist might force His people to flee there.[17]

Finally, Hutchings suggests that God and His angels may be using "orbit windows" in deep space, which science is just beginning to learn about. His proof text? Also out of context: ". . . for the windows from on high are open, and the foundations of the earth do shake" (Isaiah 24:18 KJV).[18]

Discerning the Times

Today Hutchings defends the work of the Southwest Radio Church. In an interview for this book he said that by and large Southwest has maintained integrity over the years.

"We're commanded to discern the signs of the times," he said. "We have to be credible certainly. I think for the most part this ministry has maintained a credible reputation."[19]

At this writing the Southwest Radio Church was recovering from a financial tailspin and internal strife. The Oklahoma City based ministry was producing a half-hour-long radio program, aired 5 days a week on 100 stations nationwide (down from 140) and on 40 stations, in Spanish, in South America. Founded in 1933, it is one of the oldest radio ministries in America.[20]

But in the summer of 1988, facing debts of about $700,000, the ministry's twenty-member board had removed David Webber as president and appointed Hutchings. Until his ouster, Webber had assumed control of the ministry, following his father's death in 1959. Webber, who was given a new post at the ministry, resigned in dissatisfaction several months later. But in May, 1989, he came back in a limited role as radio pastor, which includes occasionally hosting the broadcasts. In the early part of 1989 the ministry's financial condition was beginning to improve, said Hutchings.

Hutchings said that perhaps he went overboard in predicting the Jupiter Effect would cause mass destruction in 1982. If he had to do it over again, he "would put stronger qualifications in the article" that sounded the alarm of the impending Jupiter Effect. "But certainly hindsight is better than foresight," he said.

He also said he should not have pointed to Henry Kissinger as the Antichrist. "I do plead guilty to Henry Kissinger because I wrote an article pointing out the parallels. That was twelve years ago, when he first came on the scene as a great peacemaker. . . . I didn't say he was the Antichrist, I just said there were similarities. I think you can go overboard by putting the finger on everybody, and I don't really agree with that. I shouldn't have done that ten to twelve years ago."

What about all the other Antichrist candidates listed by Southwest Radio Church publications? Hutchings said he wasn't personally responsible for any of those.

What does he think of his ministry using the *National Enquirer* as a source for articles? "I don't remember ever using the *National Enquirer*. In fact, I have criticized people within the ministry for referring to it," he said.

What about the *Bible in the News*, Southwest's magazine? "I really did not have anything to do at all with that publication until lately. . . . I just would not take any responsibility for anything that was in it personally."

Marginal Mysteries

But Hutchings has been at the forefront of exploring strange topics for the radio ministry for a long time. In 1986 the ministry published his book, *Marginal Mysteries*, which included Hutchings's biblical interpretations of unexplained mysteries. Topics explored in the fifty-page book were: "Lost Atlantis, the Shroud of Turin, the Bermuda Triangle, the Mystery of the Pyramids, the Loch Ness Monster, Big Foot, the Abominable Snowman, UFOs, knowledge in the Ancient World, and the Lost Tribes of Israel." With each "marginal mystery," Hutchings has a "biblical" explanation for it.

Take the Bermuda Triangle, for example. Hutchings suggests that the mysterious area in the Atlantic Ocean (located southwest of Bermuda and northeast of the Bahama Islands), may be an area of intense satanic activity. He cites Isaiah 27:1, where God "will slay the monster of the sea," and he combines it with the tale of Jesus casting the evil spirits out of the demoniac into the swine, which ran over a cliff into the sea. The implication is that some demons have remained in the ocean from that incident, and that they may be responsible for the many missing ships and aircraft reported missing in "the Devil's Triangle."[21]

Likewise, the Abominable Snowman and Big Foot may be demons, reports Hutchings.[22] The Loch Ness monster may be one of the "sea monsters" referred to in the Bible in Lamentations 4:3 and Isaiah 27:1.[23]

Webber and Hutchings have also found a unique way of claiming that America may be "mystery Babylon," referred to in the book of Revelation:

> The identifying international emblem of the United States is the Statue of Liberty, but also nearby to the approaches to New York City on Long Island is another possible identifying symbol—Babylon. Babylon, New York, is a fairly large city made up of Babylon, North Babylon, and West Babylon, but enough to have three zip codes—11702, 11703, 11704. In fact, the entire New York City complex, long hailed as the greatest city in the world, is known as the Babylon On The Hudson.[24]

Sensational Suggestions

Webber also defended the radio ministry in a recent wide-ranging interview.[25] "I don't feel as if we've ever been sensational just to be sensational. And I don't feel like we've ever gone out on a limb as far as trying to project a definite date for the rapture or a timetable that *had* to come to pass.

"I don't think it's out of line to speculate about personalities (being the Antichrist). A lot of people were interested in Henry Kissinger because of his international peace activities. The fact is that a mathematical formula calculates his name to add up to 666. Of course you can total New York City and a lot of other things (to come up with 666) by the same formula.

"I didn't see anything we did as reckless, because we only *suggested*. Actually I think most of the time I suggested that Henry Kissinger might be a forerunner of Antichrist because of his peace-keeping abilities. I never did think he was the Antichrist; I thought he was too old. It's interesting that his father was a rabbi and came out of the Common Market countries, and this mathematical formula was interesting, but when people asked me if I thought Kissinger was the Antichrist, I always said 'No—I think he might be a forerunner of Antichrist.'

"I don't recall what we said about Waldheim or Brandt. I don't remember that. . . . As for Pope Paul, I think we brought up the fact that when he sits ex cathedra and claims to be speaking as vice-regent for God that he has the three-tiered crown, and his title equals 666 in Roman numerals. However, I have never to my knowledge suggested he could be Antichrist. To people who say, 'Do you think Rome will be the Mystery Babylon or the great whore or have to do with Antichrist?' I have only said that some future pope might be the second beast that comes up out of the earth. But I've never said that the pope or any pope would be Antichrist."

Webber explained that he has gone on record as being opposed to some Antichrist theories being propagated by the Southwest Radio Church. When Constance Cumbey was suggesting that Pat Robertson could be the Antichrist, sometimes at Southwest conferences, "I told her it was not wise for her to do so," because he didn't agree with her. He said he didn't agree with a recent book distributed by the church for a six-dollar offering that claimed Gorbachev could be the "real antichrist." In it, author Robert W. Faid claimed that the numeric figures in Gorbachev's name equaled 666 × 2.[26]

"Our Lord did admonish the religious leaders of His day for not discerning the signs of the time or the times and the seasons. So I think we should be paying attention to what the Common Market is doing, to what Russia is doing and what Israel is doing, the Arab nations and so on," Webber said. "I think we should be discerning the signs in the heavens and the earth but not feel like those signs are given specifically for the church and that we have a mandate to go out and say, 'Well you know the Lord's gonna come this year or that year or that it's gonna come to an end.'

"Because we have gone into timetables having to do with Israel, some people said to me in 1981, 'Well the Lord didn't come, what are you going to preach?' And my reply was that I never said that the Lord *had to come* in 1981, and any timetables that we suggest that have to do with Israel are *suggested timetables*. I don't think we ever said dogmatically that this timetable is rigid and will come to pass.

"I don't believe it's scriptural to set a date for the rapture; only God knows that," he concluded. "So I would say Mr.

Whisenant was not scriptural in setting a date for the rapture of the church. We've never done that and never will."

Need for a New Focus

David Webber and Noah Hutchings are two of the most likable prophecy teachers in America today. They are without a doubt committed to getting the gospel of Jesus Christ out to a dying world. A good portion of the church's printed literature, most of which is basic, orthodox teaching, is edifying. In the wake of the church's emerging from recent financial problems, the daily radio program has become more mainstream, sometimes dealing with devotional and family issues.

I just believe the Southwest Radio Church should stay away from its specialty—Bible prophecy—and stick to areas in which it is not prone to twist facts, speculate, or misrepresent Scripture.

In addition, I believe they have misused Scripture to back up many of their speculative theories. The Bible does not definitely "prove" the existence of Atlantis, sea monsters, space flight, and many other themes Southwest writers delve into.

I am also troubled by the stream of thought within the ministry that limits God. We see it with Dr. Fisher and Mr. Gaverluk's statements that the high priest in Old Testament times could have communicated with God through radio waves, transistors, and crystals. It is especially evident in Southwest's many speculations about heaven, hell, angels, and space. Their view of heaven as a physical place somewhere in the northern part of the skies, with angels scurrying back and forth between heaven and earth, limits God because it views God as a superior being instead of the Supreme Being. It also sounds like the Mormon god, who is not omnipresent, as historic Christianity teaches, but a physical being (perhaps like us) somewhere out in space. It's almost as if a strand of thought at Southwest has limited God to His creation, while orthodox Christian theology has always affirmed that God is "a personal, transcendent Creator, . . . distinct from creation."[27]

In his great wisdom, Solomon recognized that God is greater than the universe, and as he was preparing to build the temple, he lamented, " 'The temple I am going to build will be great, because our God is greater than all other gods. But who is able to build a temple for him, since the heavens, even the highest heavens, cannot contain him? Who then am I to build a temple for him, except as a place to burn sacrifices before him?' " (2 Chronicles 2:5, 6).

" 'For my thoughts are not your thoughts, neither are your ways my ways,' declares the Lord. 'As the heavens are higher than the earth, so are my ways higher than your ways and my thoughts than your thoughts' " (Isaiah 55:8, 9).

It's arrogant to pretend we understand the mysteries of the universe and His realm. Heaven is not in some supercluster somewhere in space; it is beyond our understanding. When Paul was taken to the third heaven, he couldn't describe the things he heard, and he added that if he could, he wasn't permitted to (2 Corinthians 12:4). As Psalm 8 declares: ". . . You have set your glory *above* the heavens. . . . When I consider your heavens, the work of your fingers, the moon and the stars, which you have set in place, what is man that you are mindful of him. . . ?" (Psalm 8:1, 3, 4, *emphasis added*).

Perhaps Southwest Radio Church's tendency to limit God has opened the door to even greater errors. The false presumption that God is somehow bound by His creation, bound by His cosmos, could have led to Southwest adopting a form of Christian astrology and related pyramidology, both based in the occult.

12
Consider the Source

The January/February, 1988, issue of *God's News Behind the News* magazine carried an ominous item. It quoted a Dr. Becker Frie, speaking before a gathering of scientists in West Germany: "A moon-sized object is nearing our solar system and could enter it by 1990. The object is coming toward us at 20,000 MPH—it's big and it's coming right at us."[1]

Above the quote, which was separated from the text and in bold letters, was an artist's rendition of how a planet being struck by a moon-sized object might look. The scene was mass destruction, with space debris flying about like ignited Roman candles.

The picture, however, didn't accurately portray the article's contents. Buried in the story about trends in prophecy is a quotation from an astronomer who said: "Just because it's heading for our solar system doesn't mean it's going to destroy earth." The anonymous writer of the article then went on to say that when he reads reports like that he thinks of the marvel and fear men will have some day when they see the New Jerusalem coming toward the earth from outer space.[2]

The report of the potential collision came from the sensational supermarket tabloid the *Weekly World News*. This is the kind of publication that reports on stories such as aliens impregnating children, brain transplants, or six-headed dogs, while showing the latest "Elvis is alive" photographs.

An in-depth probe of prophecy teachers in these last days shows it's not surprising for a ministry to use such a report. A whole group of teachers today appears to consistently use questionable sources for information. They may use misquotes or faulty quotes from legitimate sources, and more seriously, misquote God's Word to make it say something it clearly doesn't mean. To further reinforce their faulty theories, they quote each other to prove their points.

A Network of "Experts"

The Southwest Radio Church's March, 1989, newsletter offered several books for those supporting the radio ministry. For a gift of ten dollars, supporters would be mailed prophecy teacher Colin Deal's latest book, *Armageddon and the Twenty-First Century*. "Brother Colin Deal has published a new book presenting sound prophetic evidence that Christians may reasonably expect Christ to bring in His Kingdom upon Earth by the beginning of the seventh millennium," the newsletter states.

Just a month earlier, in his newsletter, the *End-Time News*, Colin Deal was offering David Webber and Noah Hutchings's book *New Light on the Great Pyramid*.

Down in Alabama, Mary Stewart Relfe quoted a Southwest Radio Church publication for documentation that through fiber optics our television sets will be able to spy on us.[3] She also quotes the Southwest Radio Church as inspiration for her theory that the late Anwar Sadat is the Antichrist.[4] "In appreciation" for their help in writing *When Your Money Fails*, Relfe lists the Southwest Radio Church, Colin Deal, and another prophecy teacher.

In her other book, *The New Money System*, Relfe publishes an endorsement from Patrick Fisher, an author of Southwest's Radio Church's *Fiber Optics: Eye of the Antichrist*, an exposé she quoted in her previous book. Relfe's promotional flyer advertising one of her books contains a large front-page endorsement ("ONE OF THE MOST ASTOUNDING BOOKS OF THE GENERATION") from Colin Deal. Deal also endorsed her book in Relfe's newsletter, and Relfe in the same newsletter endorsed and peddled Deal's *Christ Returns by 1988: 101 Reasons* book for a five-dollar contribution.[5]

So it goes in the world of soothsayers of the Second Advent: They endorse each other, quote each other freely, speak at various conferences together, sell each others' books, and often develop close friendships. Many have spoken at prophecy conferences in various parts of the country, sponsored by each other.

Where Did This Idea Come From?

Constance Cumbey burst upon the scene with her book *The Hidden Dangers of the Rainbow,* in 1983, creating a firestorm among evangelicals. According to Cumbey, there's a massive conspiracy underfoot to bring in the Antichrist through the New Age movement. Some of the firestorm centered around Cumbey's research and conclusions, but what really raised eyebrows was the fact she named some Christians as being part of the conspiracy. Because of Cumbey's sudden notoriety, many longtime experts in the field of cults and new religions were forced to answer questions about Cumbey's book. Among them were people who had been researching the New Age movement a lot longer than Cumbey had been, such as the Spiritual Counterfeits Project of Berkeley, California.

Although they did affirm that the New Age movement she talked about was very real and very dangerous, the immediate consensus among cult-research circles was to *reject* major portions of Cumbey's thesis. In a scene that wasn't too pretty, Cumbey was roundly criticized at a Christian Research Institute sponsored conference on the cults, in El Toro, California, in November, 1983, when she tried to defend her theories. Later the heat was turned up on her when cult expert J. Gordon Melton, author of the *Encyclopedia of American Religions*, began distributing a paper critical of Cumbey. The Saint Louis based Personal Freedom Outreach followed by publishing a tract opposing her conspiracy theories. That was followed by the reaction of the Jesus People USA (JPUSA), of Chicago, a long player in the forefront of cult research. JPUSA created a new award category in its *Cornerstone* magazine—the worst book of the year award—and presented it to *Hidden Dangers*. "Why a 'Worst Book of the Year' award. . . ?" An anonymous *Cornerstone* writer explained, "To encourage discernment in a Christian public that too often reaches to scratch their itching ears when they should be reaching for their Bibles."[6]

Despite the criticism of evangelical researchers, Cumbey became the darling of the soothsaying prophecy teachers. She landed repeated appearances on the Southwest Radio Church's daily radio program and was asked to be the featured speaker at their prophecy conferences. California prophecy teacher Charles Taylor has quoted her extensively, and Pennsylvania prophecy teacher Salem Kirban sells at least one of her books.

Within the Soothsayers' Camp

Another relative newcomer to the scene is prophecy teacher and author J. R. Church, of Oklahoma City. Church's *Hidden Prophecies in the Psalms* became a quick hit in prophecy circles.

Right now many end-time prognosticators quote Church frequently. He has become so influential that Edgar Whisenant used him as his inspiration for at least three of his 88 reasons for the rapture being in 1988 (reasons 61, 62, and 75). Henry "Watchman in the Wilderness" Kreysler claims J. R. Church's book, a tape by Colin Deal, and a page from a book by pop scientist Immanuel Velikovsky were the three factors that forced his hand to get a tape series out quickly to warn people of the rapture and great tribulation to take place in the 1990s. Charles Taylor's book *Watch 1988—The Year of Climax,* which implied a 1988 rapture, quoted Church throughout, strongly affirming his "hidden prophecies" theory.

Perhaps then, it is no coincidence that J. R. Church is now tight with the Southwest Radio Church, has hosted its radio program, and has conducted Southwest lectures.

Naming the "Experts"

Soothsayers will quote each other; and they will use pop "experts" and even quacks to substantiate their theories, but they'll seldom quote real authorities in the fields of science, economics, or theology.

To imply that her book, *The New Money System,* has the endorsement of important officials today, Mary Stewart Relfe has as her lead endorsement in the book an *unnamed* "U.S. NEWS & WORLD REPORT OFFICIAL." The alleged endorsement states: "Your book chronicles accurately the development of One World System of Government—Banking, Business and things related that need to be understood."[7] However, in reality that prestigious magazine *has not* endorsed the book. Who was the unnamed "official"? Relfe is not saying. The local circulation manager? Perhaps a secretary?

Relfe also dropped the ball in *When Your Money Fails,* as she attributed her own statements about the purpose of an Israeli lottery game to the *Jerusalem Post.* She claims the uncover-six three-times lottery is a "nationwide contest in Israel, sponsored by the Department of Education. It is designed to 'educate,' prepare and condition the Jews to accept '666,' which will be the number of their 'False Messiah' (the Antichrist), and his World Government System." For attribution of these *statements* she cited the November 25, 1980, *Jerusalem Post* that simply advertised the lottery *without comment.*[8]

Back in 1976 Doug Clark quoted unnamed "reliable

sources" to proclaim that "West Germany is now stamping people's hands . . . and this is very, very close to the description of the Mark of the Beast outlined in the Bible."[9] It's now 1989, and West Germany *has not* shifted to anything resembling a mark on the hand in order to complete financial transactions.

Bending the Word

Let's look at how some prophecy teachers have misquoted Scripture in order to "prove" their pet theories.

Colin Deal says:

- That despite Jesus' telling us in Matthew 24:36 that we are not to know the day or hour of His return, He still intends for us to know through other means when He's coming back. To prove it, Deal quotes Jesus, in John 16:12: "I have much more to say to you, more than you can now bear."[10] Obviously, however, Jesus was not referring to His Second Coming in this verse.
- That the PTL television network's satellite could be the angel described in Revelation 14:6. That Scripture passage, referring to the tribulation, talks about an ". . . angel flying in midair, and he had the eternal gospel to proclaim to those who live on the earth—to every nation, tribe, language and people."[11] Obviously, a satellite is not an angel, and there are many satellites transmitting the gospel today.
- That Jesus claimed there would be 153 nations on earth at the time of His coming. Deal reasoned that there were 153 fishes in the net pulled to land in John 21:11. In Matthew 13:47–49, when Christ compared the kingdom of heaven to a net cast into a sea and pulled to shore at the end of the world, Deal claims that it means there would be 153 nations—an amount comparable to the count in the 1980s.[12] (Using this method of Bible interpretation, one could prove almost any wild presupposition with Scripture.)
- That Revelation 6:8 predicts that chemical warfare will be used during a future Russian invasion. That text states: "I

looked, and there before me was a pale horse! Its rider was named Death, and Hades was following close behind him. They were given power over a fourth of the earth to kill by sword, famine and plague, and by the wild beasts of the earth." Deal reasoned that the Greek term for *pale* in the verse is *chlorous,* and that means "yellowish-green." He then claims that's what poison gas looks like.[13] But there are flaws to this. The verse can mean *many other things* than chemical warfare. To assume the Russian army is somehow associated with the text is definitely reading into the text something that simply isn't there.

Deal is not the only one who has used the Bible this way. Southwest Radio Church publications:

- Have used the book of Job (18:4 and 18:15) to "prove" the existence of Atlantis. Here is the highly speculative reasoning. Notice the passages say nothing about an ancient civilization—or any civilization.

  We read in Job 18:4, *"He teareth himself in his anger: shall the earth be forsaken for thee? and shall the rock be removed out of his place?"* the rock (the earth) was moved so that the righteous would not again be corrupted, as they had been preceding the Flood. We read in Job 18:15, *"It shall dwell in his tabernacle, because it is none of his: brimstone shall be scattered upon his habitation."* The splitting of the earth could be achieved by showers of ash and volcanic fire. When part of the world broke away, the other part received a fearful jolt, and this affected their national identity. It is certainly worth pondering and applying.[14]

- Ignored the biblical record that Elijah hid in a cave in Mount Sinai following his confrontation with Jezebel.

  David Webber and Noah Hutchings claimed that Elijah hid in the rock city of Petra, now in Jordan, which is about 180 miles northeast of Mount Sinai. Their reasoning? "Scripture indicated that Petra will be the place of refuge for the faithful remnant of Israel when they flee from the Antichrist

. . . it may be at this time that he [Elijah, now resurrected as one of the two witnesses referred to the book of Revelation] will personally lead the remnant to the same location where he found refuge from Jezebel." The authors then claim that although "tradition indicates that the cave was on Mt. Sinai [which is also called Mt. Horeb] . . . our position" is that Elijah hid at "Petra."[15]

Webber and Hutchings are mistaken, though. It wasn't tradition that stated the cave was at Mount Horeb. It's clearly in the Bible (1 Kings 19:8). Scripture also doesn't indicate that the Jews will flee to Petra during the tribulation (though it's possible they will). That's an assumption propagated by Southwest and other prophecy ministries.

13
Many Dare Call It Conspiracy

Adolf Hitler thought every German should have a copy of *The Protocols of the Learned Elders of Zion*. The Nazis distributed the book throughout the Reich because they thought it highlighted the Jewish "menace." The book, first presented to the czar of Russia in 1903, charged the Jews with a conspiracy to destroy society and take over the world.[1]

The *Protocols* have long since been discredited as pure nonsense and a "grotesque forgery."[2] Still, the book won't go away. Wherever anti-Semitic hate has reared its ugly head, the *Protocols* seemed to have been there first. The insidious book was distributed to the White Russian army, which used it to blame—and later massacre—the Jews for the 1917 revolution. Today in America you can find the *Protocols;* it's a key document in the Neo-Nazi and Identity ("Christian") movements.

One prophecy ministry draws on it, too. But the Midnight Cry Publishing Company of Tequesta, Florida, publishers of literature on Bible prophecy for more than fifty years, *does not* give credence to the *Protocols'* anti-Semitic ideas. *Cry* editors acknowledge it is a forgery, but blame its creation on a conspiracy headed by the "Illuminati." It was purposely written to make the Jews and Masons "scapegoats" while the "Illuminati" (working through the New Age movement) tries to take over the world and bring the Antichrist to power, they allege.[3]

Searching for Conspiracy

Is there a worldwide conspiracy underway to unite the world under Satan's dictator, the Antichrist? Is an organization called the Illuminati behind the scenes, pulling the strings? After exploring these questions for a long time, reading almost every book I could get my hands on concerning the conspiracy and the Illuminati, I have not found any evidence that such an organization exists today.

Historical records show that an organization called the Illuminati *did* exist. It was founded by Adam Weishaupt on May 1, 1776, and government leaders in America and Europe referred to it just after the American Revolution. One of the purposes of the organization was to create a new world order. But European governments were warned of the plans, and in 1785, the Bavarian government seized Weishaupt's papers and exposed the conspiracy, which was very small. According to everything I've read about the Illuminati, it disappeared a short time later. Some, however, say it resurfaced in the 1800s under a different name. Even if that *is* true, no proof has surfaced that it continued beyond the 1880s.

Some prophecy teachers have argued that it continues today under different names, such as the Trilateral Commission, of which Jimmy Carter, George Bush, Henry Kissinger, and many other leaders are (or once were) a part. Many say the Council on Foreign Relations (CFR), which has as its members many banking, media, and political leaders, is a major part of it. Others say it has manifested itself in the United Nations. But the truth is that we don't have solid evidence that any of these modern unifying forces have their roots in a centuries-old man-made conspiracy.

Many prophecy teachers either have taught or are teaching the existence of a conspiracy headed by an Illuminati organization that is poising mankind to accept a one-world government. Some have already unwisely supported baseless notions and fraudulent imposters. Salem Kirban and Doug Clark, for example, were fooled by a man named John Todd who criss-crossed America in the 1970s, speaking at many churches (often with a loaded gun in his holster and with rifle-toting bodyguards). Todd frightened fundamentalist Christians everywhere, teaching an Illuminati conspiracy headed by satanists and witches had already taken over many Christian organizations and at least one evangelical denomination. He stated that an upheaval would strike America in 1979, that Jimmy Carter was the Antichrist, and that his late sister Ruth Carter Stapleton was a high priestess of witchcraft. The murder and torture of Christians would begin soon, and he added that Christian leaders were part of the conspiracy. He claimed Jerry Falwell was bought off for a $50 million check, that he (Todd) funneled $8 million to Chuck Smith of Calvary Chapel while he was a witch working for the Illuminati, and that Full Gospel Businessmen leader Demos Shakarian was a leading figure in the Illuminati.[4]

Well, Ed Plowman, formerly of *Christianity Today*, and others eventually exposed Todd as a fraud with a police record, who had served prison time for corrupting the morals of children and had undergone psychological care. Todd "stormed out" of the Melodyland Christian Center in Anaheim, California, amid accusations—that were also voiced in other places—that he was seducing young girls.[5] The issue in which Plowman reported this also contained an editorial about Todd: "Considerable evidence suggests Todd to be a sick man who must be helped before someone is shot to death. He has exploited and abused those who have believed in him. What is needed is for people to stop believing in him so that he can be helped."

Todd was thrust into the limelight after hooking up with Doug Clark and appearing on his "Amazing Prophecies" show.[6] Many in those days—and many prophecy teachers in particular—believed Todd's fantastic story without investigating any of it.

Salem Kirban also furthered Todd's "career" before he was exposed. In a 1978 issue of *Salem Kirban's Jerusalem Report,* he wrote that Todd's testimony "is the most shocking message I have ever heard." He then talked about Todd's accusations and offered one of Todd's tapes, along with a detailed report, for an offering. "I believe every Christian should have this report," Kirban wrote.[7]

Around that same time Kirban began inserting sections into some of his books about the conspiracy and the Illuminati. His 1980 book, *Satan's Angels Exposed,* devoted a chapter to the Illuminati, while much of the rest of the book developed the idea of a massive conspiracy underway to control the world.

Southwest Radio Church later cited Kirban's research. But after Plowman exposed Todd, Southwest distributed copies of the article to try to counteract the fear Todd was responsible for. Southwest also never let Todd be a guest on the daily radio program.

Fact or Theory?

Another author talking about an unfolding world-conquering (or uniting, depending on whose side you are on) conspiracy today is Texe Marrs, author of a number of books on the New Age movement and Bible prophecy. In Marrs's 1988 book, *Mystery Mark of the New Age,* he asserts "some New Agers have already taken the Mark [of the Beast]!"[8] The book also asserts that Gorbachev is a New Ager and that he has an active part in a New Age conspiracy that may result in the coronation of the Antichrist.

Those alleging conspiracy scenarios for the last days should be careful to say it's a theory only. Kirban, who has probably written more about the Illuminati conspiracy than any other prophecy teacher, today says he's not sure if Satan is orchestrating a demonic hidden conspiracy that no human can get a firm grasp on or whether there are human leaders knowingly working toward it. "Time will tell," he said in his statement to me. "I do not dwell on the conspiratorial view but do occasionally write on the subject to show that Satan is a deceiver and master planner who works through his agents on earth."[9] No other prophecy teachers contacted had concrete proof that the Illuminati exist today.

If these conspiracy theories are designed to frighten us about the horror just ahead, then they are not of God. Such fear mongering is specifically condemned in the Bible, which tells us to cling to the Lord instead. Isaiah 8:12–14 states: " 'Do not call conspiracy everything that these people call conspiracy; do not fear what they fear, and do not dread it. The Lord Almighty is the one you are to regard as holy, he is the one you are to fear, he is the one you are to dread, and he will be a sanctuary. . . .' "

Finally, we should be mindful that mankind is already involved in a conspiracy—a conspiracy of rebellion—against God, and many don't realize it. Just because many people don't see themselves as knowing, active conspirators doesn't mean they aren't involved. Psalm 2:1, 2 states: "Why do the nations rage and the peoples plot in vain? The kings of the earth take their stand and the rulers gather together against the Lord and against his Anointed One."

It's the same conspiracy that began in the Garden of Eden thousands of years ago, when Satan tempted Eve.

14
The Ultimate Date Setter?

Charles Taylor has been teaching Bible prophecy for a long time. He started as a teenager, in 1932, teaching prophecy to junior high school youths. Since then, through his Today in Bible Prophecy ministry, Taylor has grown to become one of the most influential prophecy teachers in America.

These days, however, he's on a downslide. He has had to cancel his weekly prophecy program on the PTL cable network and scale back his *Bible Prophecy News* magazine. In a recent interview he said he is on just six television stations (down from dozens of stations years ago) and a weekly program on Reverend Jerry Falwell's LBN cable network.

Taylor, a gray-haired quick-talking man, knows that over the years many have accused him of being an unscriptural date setter. Lately he's come under fire from some for his increasingly bold assertions that King Juan Carlos of Spain is the Antichrist. But Taylor, in a wide-ranging interview with me, defended himself. (Many of Taylor's thoughts in this chapter are from that same interview.) Taylor is very friendly and willing to talk at great length about his beliefs. The main point he made is that he's not a date setter; many have simply misunderstood him over the years, he said.[1]

"I don't have a problem with what I've said, but with

what people *say* I've said. . . . I simply identified the things that were happening in relation to the order of events and what the likelihood would be of Him coming at that time, but I never declared that that was the time that He was coming. God is supreme; you know, we don't tell Him what to do."[2]

Taylor *does* admit suggesting a number of time periods for the rapture and that most of these dates revolve around a theme he has been preaching for a long time: that Jesus will rapture His church during the Jewish Feast of Trumpets just prior to a seven-year tribulation time period. That's also a theme familiar to other prophecy teachers, such as Edgar Whisenant. But Taylor says that's not date setting. "If a date is mentioned, people jump right down your throat and say, 'Hey, you set a date.' Well, that's not setting a date if you just let them know when the Feast of Trumpets is and give the reasons why it is in the realm of possibility that this could be the year of its happening."[3]

Taylor also defends pointing to King Juan Carlos as the Antichrist. When asked what happens if the Spanish monarch is not the future world dictator, Taylor said, "I think there's no possibility of it being anybody else. Absolutely, and I say that from a Bible standpoint. Daniel 7:8 and 24—he will uproot three and so forth and there will be the final ten [nations] that continue through the tribulation period, but it's a revised ten, and that's exactly what's happening in the Common Market."

The Boy Who Cried Wolf?

What then can we make of Charles Taylor? Can he be faulted for his views? Is he a date setter? Is he a sensationalist? Has he slandered King Juan Carlos?

After examining much of Taylor's work since 1974, questions arise concerning his predictions. In many cases Taylor not only suggested a specific year when Jesus would rapture the church, but at times almost *guaranteed it*. Another problem is that almost *every year* Taylor goes on record as saying this is probably the year of the rapture—and eleven times he has done that.

Such repeated predictions are not unlike the story of the boy crying wolf so often that when the real wolf came, no one believed him. After his numerous Feast of Trumpets "rapture watch" failures, some got discouraged. Taylor himself has written about the discouragement, yet he keeps up the practice annually. He repeatedly appeals to people to give to his ministry, using the upcoming rapture date as an incentive. Wrote Taylor in September 1980:

> We don't have another decade. Many believe, as I do, that now we most likely have less than one year in which to reach the lost of this nation (and the world.) . . . All gifts are tax deductible, but what will it matter if you are "caught up" into heaven or blown to———? It's just that serious.[4]

Let's look at some of Taylor's statements on the rapture. Could it be that Taylor is America's ultimate date setter, without mentioning the "day and hour" of Christ's return, or has he been misunderstood? You decide.

A Suggested 1975 Rapture. "Since each jubilee era is seven weeks of years (49 years), the prophetic period to be anticipated is 69 × 49 = 3,381 years. . . . To get the prophetic Gregorian calendar year, subtract the number of years before Christ. This gives us the following equation: 3,381 − 1406 = 1975! This could mean the renewal of Jewish time, the close of the Church Age and 'THE RAPTURE OF THE CHURCH.' "[5]

"In the Hebrew year 5736, it [Trumpets] will come on September 6, 1975. And that day is a Sabbath day and it also is the last year in 'this generation' which would still allow the seven-year Tribulation Period to close by the year 1983.

". . . We do not dare to predict that this is the God-ordained date for the rapture of the Church, but we cannot help but to note that all of the revealed prophecies pertaining to our Lord's return would be fulfilled."[6]

"WILL SEPTEMBER 6, 1975, BE THE DATE OF THE FULFILLMENT OF THE FEAST OF TRUMPETS in which 'The Lord himself shall descend from heaven with a shout, with the voice of the archangel and with the trump of God' to catch away His body of believers in the rapture of the Church? WE CAN ONLY SAY THAT THERE IS OVERWHELMING EVIDENCE THAT THIS COULD BE THE DAY."[7]

Suggested 1976 Rapture. "Since there are 35 years in a Bible generation, it is easy to calculate the end of 'this generation': 1948 plus 35 equals 1983. This becomes the year in which all things must be consummated, including the return of Christ in power and glory at the end of the seven-year Tribulation. To arrive at the maximum date for the rapture of the Church, we must subtract seven years from 1983 which puts us back to 1976. Is this the year of the rapture? It could happen even sooner. . . ."[8]

Suggested 1980 Rapture. "Since '70' is so significant in Jewish prophecy, there is a theory that 70 years after the Balfour Declaration, Israel will have its sovereignty and peace. Messiah will come. If this holds true, and Jesus comes as Messiah the King in 1987 (1917 + 70 = 1987): on that basis, His return for His Body, the Church, would be seven years prior—in 1980. This is possible."[9]

". . . A 40-year span, a generation, from the rebirth of Israel as a nation on May 14, 1948 brings us to May 14, 1988. Subtracting the seven years of Tribulation that places us at May 1981. The Rosh Hashana—Feast of Trumpets—previous to that date brings us right back to Sept. 11, 1980. Could this be the appointed time for the Rapture of the Church?"[10]

Suggested 1981 Rapture (if 1980 Fails). "If Jesus doesn't come on Feast of Trumpets (Sept. 10) of this year [1980], we probably will have one more year to serve Him here on Earth."[11]

Then in the October, 1980, newsletter the next month, Taylor firmed up his new date: "The order of events in line with specific prophecies of the Bible indicate we probably have just one more year before the holocaust."[12]

Suggested 1982 Rapture. "If it [rapture] occurs at the time of the Feast of Trumpets, as many Bible scholars teach, it would be in September. Will it be in September of 1982? Only God in heaven knows for sure, but a study of documented news from the world scene certainly points in that direction."[13]

Suggested 1983 Rapture. "Three nations are likely to be dropped [from the European Common Market]—just as prophesied in the Bible. . . . THIS COULD BE THE YEAR [1983], for all groups and nations now are aligning as prophesied."[14] "Now the time has come to warn all people and to alert them to the fact that JESUS IS COMING SOON."[15]

Suggested 1985 Rapture. "That would move up the time period for the rapture of the church to the middle of September, which coincides with the Feast of Trumpets, September 15–16, 1985. Could this be THE YEAR? The order of events indicate that everything is virtually ready. Are You?"[16]

A Firm 1986 Rapture? "It is self-evident, therefore, that we now are standing at the very end of the Church Age. That which you and I desire to do for the cause of Christ we must do it NOW. Any souls we want to win or any service we hope to do, WE MUST DO IT NOW, FOR JESUS IS COMING SOON. And I do not mean in a few years: it now is a matter of months or only of weeks! GIVE OF YOUR BEST TO THE MASTER TODAY!!

". . . By the time of the Feast of Trumpets of this year (Oct. 4) [1986], it is possible that the President of the EC will be in full power and be in favor of signing the prophesied 7-year treaty, and we'll be gone!"[17]

"June 25, 1986 Assoc. Press: LONDON—Syria is planning a limited war with Israel LATER THIS YEAR to regain the disputed Golan Heights . . . The trigger of the war undoubtedly will be the rapture of the church. . . . We may have only a year or two, or even have only a few months left in which to reach our loved ones."[18]

Suggested 1987 Rapture. "If the Jewish people in Israel proclaim Jubilee and physically take possession of the Temple site on next Day of Atonement, Oct. 3, 1987, it will cause such strife. . . . Rosh Hashana, the Feast of Trumpets, in 1987, will be 10 days before the Day of Atonement, as always, occurring Sept. 24, 1987. Will that be the day of the Rapture? All signs point to it, although only God knows for sure."[19]

"The exciting book 'Watch 1986' no longer is available. We are sold out! As you read this, I'm rushing the new book 'Watch 1987' through the printers. . . . 1987 looks like 'the' year for many biblical reasons."[20]

A 1988 Rapture. "Now a proven friend of the Jewish people and nation, King Juan Carlos is about 'ready' to become the powerful leader of the pro-Israel revived Roman empire, and we are about ready to be 'caught up' to our heavenly home! September of 1988?"[21]

"This new book [*Watch 1988—The Year of Climax*] is being written with the expectation that it will be the last book I will ever write on earth. . . . With the millennial reign of Christ due to begin in 1995 (see page 10) [where he quotes the last-days timetable given by prophecy teacher J. R. Church], the rapture must surely occur in 1988 to coordinate with many other prophecies."[22]

"Will YOU be ready when the Lord comes to take us to Glory 'in the twinkling of an eye?' Expect it to happen this September!"[23]

A 1989 Rapture. "Because Jesus did not come on Feast of Trumpets in 1988, however, some have become discouraged. . . . It appears that we have another year in which to serve our Lord."[24] "Judging from the maximum of that time period, Sept. 29, 1996, the rapture of the church should take place seven years prior—by Feast of Trumpets and Rosh Hashana of 1989—by Sept. 30, 1989!"[25]

Taylor is quick to admit that many prophecy teachers, sparked by excitement over the possibility that Jesus is coming back soon, have misinterpreted the signs of the times and have read too much into news events. He said the way to avoid prophecy error is to see the world's events in the light of Scripture and "compare Scripture (verses) with (other) Scripture (verses)."

In explaining his reasons for believing the Jupiter Effect was a legitimate threat, he conceded, "There was a little too much excitement about it. . . . They went off the deep end as some people did and said that because of those earthquakes the Lord's going to come. It's not proper to do that, you see."

Why then do so many prophecy teachers look at the world events and incorrectly find end-times scenarios for them? "Well, people are anxious for the Lord to come, and they grab at straws. This is what has happened in many instances," he explained. But Taylor would not place himself in that category, though he seems to fit the criteria. Take Taylor's use of Ezekiel 37 and 38, for example, some of the most-cited passages by today's prophecy teachers. Taylor seems to find cryptic messages in the passages that deal with a future invasion of Israel by Gog and Magog, which is commonly identified as the Soviet Union today.

In *WATCH 1988—The Year of Climax*, Taylor wrote that the prophetic Gog had formed in 1985:

> Did you notice, by-the-way, that in 1985 the prophesied G-O-G came into reality when Andrei Gromyko was elevated to President of the Soviet Union, when Marshall Nikolai Ogarkov became head of the Warsaw Pact and Soviet Armies; and when Mikhail Gorbachev became the General Secretary of the Communist Party of the Soviet Union? . . . Yes, BIBLE PROPHECY IS BEING FULFILLED IN GREAT MEASURE AND IN

> GREAT SPECIFIC DETAIL EXACTLY AS WRITTEN IN THE BIBLE, and this could very well be THE YEAR OF CLIMAX![26]

But a short time after publication of the book, Gromyko was ousted from his long-term leadership position. (Gorbachev strengthened his position by assuming several other titles, including the presidency.) Taylor, barely skipping a beat, in print and on his television program, began claiming that Gorbachev's name stood for GOG!

> With the Moslems ready to declare all-out holy war (Jihad) and with GOGrbachev (Russian spelling for Gorbachev) in much greater power position today and King Juan Carlos of Spain taking his proper position as the next chairman of the Common Market on January 1, 1989, all the loose ends seem to be coming to climax."[27]

Does the correct spelling of Gorbachev in Russian actually begin with *Gog*, as Taylor claims? Alexander Bobilev, a University of Pennsylvania faculty lecturer in Slavic studies, laughed when he saw Taylor's assertion. "He's making that up," said the Russian-studies instructor, adding that Gorbachev's name is spelled the same in the Russian language, with one exception—the *ch* in English is one letter in the Soviet language.[28]

Charles Taylor went beyond the bounds of sound biblical interpretation of prophecy in 1979, when he predicted that the late Anwar Sadat of Egypt would soon sound "the starting gun of World War III" by invading Israel. "This will take place only when ordered by the Kremlin, for the Russians are to make the next move."[29] He then suggested that Americans should head for the hills. Nuclear war was coming, which might cause southern California to sink into the ocean!

> It would be most advisable not to locate near any known earthquake fault, and especially not to live

> west of the San Andreas fault in California [where Taylor himself lives in southern California]. Heavy concentrations of thermonuclear blasts on the West Coast due to the many strategic targets, such as army, navy and marine bases, and also many aircraft and electronic and other war-related industries located there could very easily knock off the entire West Coast shelf causing that area to sink below the sea.[30]

But as history records, Sadat wound up a courageous peacemaker with Israel and a martyr. He also all but eliminated Russian influence from Egypt. When Sadat was assassinated in 1981, Taylor changed his tune again, as outlined in a subsequent book, *Death of Sadat . . . Start of World War III.* In that book he claims that Sadat's assassination "sent a shockwave throughout the Middle East and around the world. It brought about changes that rapidly will lead to World War III. . . . Before long, you can expect Mubarak to join forces with the other Arabs in a jihad (Moslem holy war) to take these areas, and all of Israel by force."[31]

History has proven him wrong once again. Another claim in the book, triggered by the Sadat assassination, of a superpower war, also hasn't happened: "As predicted in the Bible, the USA will fight the USSR in a violent nuclear war."[32] The Scripture verses about Gog and Magog predict a war with Israel, not a *nuclear war* between the superpowers. That's not to say America won't duke it out with the Russians someday; there is that possibility, but it can't be proven with Scripture.

As the boy who cried wolf, Taylor is losing his audience. He is no longer believable.

There is little reason to suspect he has bad motives. Taylor is genuinely all excited that "Jesus is coming soon." If his zeal becomes tempered with restraint, he could rechannel his efforts in the direction of evangelism and use his knowledge of prophecy to reap a harvest of souls.

15
Fire and Brimstone

The pizza ovens were running hot that summer night in 1975. Scores of customers had called in orders, and we were working double time, sprinkling on the cheese and pepperoni, trying to catch up that hot night. I was working as a sometime pizza chef and oven man on the weekends, paying my way through college. I still remember with fondness the wonderful aromas that used to float out of that quaint little Italian restaurant and pizza shop.

On the other side of the pizza kitchen that night was Jeff, and I knew something was troubling him; he clearly wasn't concentrating. You could see fear on his face, and I knew I was indirectly to blame for it.

In my newly saved zeal I had brought a copy of evangelist David Wilkerson's new book *The Vision* to work with me that day. Before we got busy that afternoon, he had buried his face into it, read most of it within two hours. I could tell he was troubled over the book's message that within a decade America and the rest of the world would begin to fall apart and that we were soon to face terrifying judgments.

What Wilkerson, the author of the multimillion-copy best-seller *The Cross and the Switchblade,* claimed in his new book was that God gave him a terrifying vision of doomsday in the summer of 1973. He wrote that most of the coming events he described would take place "soon" and "within the next few years."[1] He added, "I have received only a hazy glimpse beyond the next decade. . . . the world economy will continue in confusion until the time of the Antichrist."[2] In the last part of the book he talked about the coming terrors of the great tribulation of the Bible, which he said would come later and are separate from his vision.

What did Wilkerson see? "A vision of five tragic calamities coming upon the earth. While I was in prayer late one night, these visions of world calamities came over me with such impact that I could do nothing but kneel, transfixed, and take it all in."[3]

I remember feeling very victorious that night, when during the first break we got, Jeff went into the men's room by himself and, scared to death, asked Jesus Christ to come into his life and save him from the horrors to come.

Visions of the Future?

I, too, remember being frightened when I first read the book. In those early years after Hal Lindsey's *The Late Great Planet Earth,* many young Christians like myself were wolfing down prophecy books at a rapid clip. *The Vision* had confirmed in my mind what I thought the future would hold. It seemed to closely match what Lindsey wrote, and I believed it.

I remember arguing with my father over the book. My dad, a Bible-believing United Methodist minister, had urged me to take the book with a grain of salt. Thinking I had become wise since I had gotten saved, about a year before that, I wouldn't take his advice. How could we *not* believe it? I argued. *The Vision* was coming from *David Wilkerson,* the same David Wilkerson played by Pat Boone in the movie *The Cross and the Switchblade,* who fearlessly went into New York City and led some of the toughest gang members to Christ.

"So what?" he said, undaunted. Man was still fallible.

It turns out—as it often does—that my dad was right. Do

you know many people today driving around in a twenty-year-old car? That's what would have happened to me if I had followed Wilkerson's advice in the book. He said things were going to deteriorate so rapidly that we had to stay debt free and prepare to flee to the country. "Get a good reliable car and stick with it," he wrote. "Don't anticipate trading it for a good, long while. Hold on to it!"[4]

Recently I lost touch with Jeff. But I heard he became discouraged over the "Christian business." He also wasn't about to believe Christians who talked about the end of the age anymore, I heard. He had gotten that way because he had become discouraged with Wilkerson. So had I.

Many of Wilkerson's prophecies did not come true, and he personally urged skeptical readers to test his vision, as the Scriptures rightly tell us to do *every time* a prophet speaks a message he claims is from God:

> I repudiate the idea that this vision is a "fear-mongering" message. . . . *Its message can be tested only by time and events.* God will be the judge and nothing my friends or enemies say can hinder me in my course to warn readers that these things be true.[5]

Here are some of the prophecies that failed the test of time and events:

- There would be "worldwide economic confusion just ahead" that would strike Europe, then the Americas, Japan, and elsewhere. It would hit the Arab countries especially hard.[6]
- The years following 1973 would be very prosperous, and people would spend unconcernedly. For a few years, the economy would prosper.[7] (In reality, economic recession began in 1974, followed by the oil crisis in America. Much of the western world—and the Arab countries—has prospered during the 1980s.)
- "The most tragic earthquake in its history" would rock the United States. It might not take place in California, but in a place where it would be least expected.[8]

- American food reserves would dwindle—in part as a result of drought and floods.[9]
- More than one-third of the United States would be designated a disaster area within the next few years.[10]
- Within ten years, South America would turn into a "powder keg, exploding in all directions."[11]
- Drastic weather changes would occur, causing unbelievable hailstorms that would cause destruction and death.[12]
- In the cities, homosexual mobs would attack children on the streets.[13]
- A new black-market sex drug would be sold to young people. It would break down their morals and lead them into promiscuity. Marijuana would be made legal.[14]
- The Roman Catholic Church would no longer welcome those who had Pentecostal leanings. The pope would take a stand against the charismatic movement.[15]

Fulfillment of Prophecy

Wilkerson did mention some things in the book that came true. He did claim there was a "flood of filth" coming—pornography would first come into our living rooms via cable television, then progress in movies after midnight, and then on almost any time of day. Don't laugh. Take a look at today's daytime soap operas.

He also mentioned that "new epidemics" would come—before the discovery of AIDS. But in the same paragraph he listed that there would be a major cholera epidemic sweeping through various underdeveloped countries—something that didn't happen.

Many things about Wilkerson's ministry are beneficial to the body of Christ. His effective work with recovering drug addicts is certainly to be commended, along with the impact of his best-selling book *The Cross and the Switchblade*, which has powerfully touched many lives. In addition Wilkerson is furious with sin in the church. In *The Vision* he wrote that God is going to judge Christians for their "secret sins," and he rightly said God is going to judge many for sins of omission.

However, using the Scriptures as our criterion, we see that he has not had a perfect track record, and perhaps fear has appeared to overwhelm a gospel message.

Wilkerson has continued to prophesy since *The Vision* and has a brand new set of prophetic claims. In his latest book, *Set the Trumpet by Thy Mouth—Hosea 8:1*, he has compared himself to Amos and Ezekiel.[16] He makes yet another startling claim for himself: He is God's "trumpet" to the world today warning it of impending destruction. This time he doesn't care who believes him:

> How they will scoff and laugh at this message. Theologians will reject it because they can't fit it into their doctrine. The pillow prophets of peace and prosperity will publicly denounce it.
>
> I no longer care. God has made my face like flint and put steel in my backbone. I am blowing the Lord's trumpet with all my might. Let the whole world and all the church call me crazy, but I must blow the trumpet and awaken God's people.[17]

What does Wilkerson say God is telling him to proclaim? "America is going to be destroyed by fire!" A soon, sudden, all-out nuclear attack from the Soviet Union is the method God will use, he wrote. "Sudden destruction is coming and few will escape. Unexpectedly, and in one hour, a hydrogen holocaust will engulf America—and this nation will be no more."[18] He also claimed that after the strike, the Soviet Union will also be judged by fire.

Before that America will face an economic collapse: "Soon, very soon, an economic nightmare will explode into reality. What frightful news it will be! 'O thou that dwellest upon many waters, abundant in treasures, thine end is come, and the measure of thy covetousness' (Jeremiah 51:13 [KJV]). America is about to face a time of mass hysteria, as banks close and financial institutions crumble and our economy spins totally out of control."[19] He also claims America is Babylon, referred to in Revelation 18.

I'm not about to say that America *won't be* destroyed someday. God has blessed America with wealth, prestige, and power. He has placed the United States in a position to send the gospel to the nations and to feed and help a suffering and dying world. The nation was founded on God's Word and His principles.

Today America exports violence, filth, and false religions to the rest of the world. Americans have killed more than 20 million babies through abortion, since 1973—more than three times the number of Jews that died in Hitler's ovens. Indeed, America may be destroyed soon. Didn't Jesus say "to whom much is given, much is required"? Didn't God use heathen empires in Old Testament times to bring down Israel for the same reasons He may bring down America?

We need good men who are willing to take a stand against sin, who are not afraid to call a spade a spade when it comes to America's stand before God. Those who forthtell the judgment that will fall on anyone who does not believe in God and follow Him are doing much to alert our nation to the need for turning away from sin.

Certainly we need to appreciate Wilkerson's intolerance of sin and his desire to call people to righteousness. I have no problem with his proclamation of judgment. But it is one thing to declare that God will punish sin, and it is another to say when He is scheduled to do it.

Apocalypse Now?

Wilkerson is by no means the only one in recent years to have apocalyptic visions. In recent days Aquilla Wilkins, a so-called prophetess from Texas, has been on both the Christian Broadcasting Network's "700 Club" and TBN's "Praise the Lord" show, talking about her visions of tough times, which she claims will start around 1992.

Are visions for today? It's hard to say. The book of Joel tells us that in the last days ". . . your sons and daughters will prophesy, your old men will dream dreams, your young men will see visions" (Joel 2:28). But the trouble is that many of these end-time visions of America—all given by supposedly Spirit-filled men and women—differ dramatically from each other. Could it be that some of today's visionaries have placed divine meaning on their own thoughts?

Christian writer Frank Hammond's vision, for example, claims that God told him that judgment was coming to America, but that it "would NOT be the result of war and foreign invasion. The 'nation' that comes against us is to be a demonic kingdom."[20] He claims an economic collapse is coming soon.

The late Roxanne Brant also saw no fiery demise of America in war as Wilkerson claims. She claimed she saw the southern half of Florida sinking into the ocean. For that reason she bought a vast chunk of land for the Roxanne Brant Ministries in northern Florida, claiming that "many other coast lands of this country and the world" may be under water "within this generation."[21] She died in 1986.

In the early 1980s Dr. James McKeever used to run transcripts of visions sent to him from other Christians in his *End Times News Digest* newsletter. One, which ran in the February, 1982, issue, claimed war with Russia would come before the end of 1983. Another vision, published in April, 1982, claimed that the great tribulation would begin "within weeks."

McKeever says he doesn't run such prophecies or visions of others anymore in his newsletter. "I've gotten wiser," he said. "I would really have to feel a very strong leading of the Lord to include one now."[22]

In all, I think my dad's advice of fifteen years ago is pretty good for today: Take all extrabiblical visions and prophecies of the end with a grain of salt. Tough times ahead or not, it shouldn't matter to us. If we're living every day as if it could be our last, proclaiming the gospel as we go, we'll have no reason to fear what's ahead. Besides that, let's stick with what we've been told about the future in God's Word. That is infallible.

[illegible] But the trouble is that that your [illegible] —all got on by supposedly [illegible] —almost automatically [illegible]. Could it be that some of today's visionaries have placed [illegible] meaning on their own thoughts?

Christian writer Frank [illegible] vision, for example claims that God told him that judgment was coming to America, but that it would not be the result of war and foreign invasion [illegible] is to be a [illegible] economic collapse is coming [illegible]

The late Roxanne Brant also saw [illegible] demise of America as well as Wilkerson did. She claimed she saw the southern half of Florida sinking into the ocean. For that reason she bought a vast amount of land for the Roxanne Brant Ministries in north [illegible] Florida, claiming that "many other coastal lands of this country and the world" may be under water "within this generation." She died in 1986.

In the early 1980s Dr. James McKeever used to run transcripts of visions sent to him from other Christians in his [illegible] Times Advisor newsletter, [illegible] which ran in the February 1982 issue, claimed war with Russia would come before the end of 1982. Another vision, published in April 1982, claimed that the great tribulation would begin "within weeks."

McKeever says he doesn't [illegible] such prophecies or visions of others anywhere in his newsletter. "I've gotten wiser," he said. "I would really have to have a very strong leading of the Lord to include one now."

In all, I think my dad's advice of fifty years ago is pretty good for today. Take all extrabiblical visions and prophecies of the end with a grain of salt. Though [illegible] ahead cannot [illegible] it shouldn't matter to us. If we're living every day as if it could be our last, [illegible] the Gospel as we go, we'll [illegible] that [illegible] with what we're told about the future in God's Word. That's enough for me.

Part IV
Crediting the Occult and Other Questionable Practices

Despite their many orthodox beliefs, some soothsayers have frequently appealed to such occult practices as astrology, numerology, and pyramidology in their end-time visions.

The word *occult* means "hidden," and such soothsayers seek knowledge hidden from others as they attempt to see into the prophecies of the Bible. In so doing they have—knowingly or unwittingly—defied Scripture's clear commands.

The word the Bible uses to describe such actions is *divination*, which means "the practice of seeking to foresee the future or discover hidden knowledge." Scripture warns: "Let no one be found among you who . . . practices divination or . . . interprets omens . . ." (Deuteronomy 18:10).

How can you tell a diviner when you see one? Zechariah says, ". . . Diviners see visions that lie, they tell dreams that are false. They give comfort in vain. Therefore the people wander like sheep oppressed for lack of a shepherd" (10:2).

God takes false prophecy seriously. He, who commanded that Israel should have no other gods and warned them of his jealousy (Exodus 20:3, 5), proclaims, ". . . I am the Lord, who has made all things, who alone stretched out the heavens, who spread out the earth by myself, who foils the signs of false prophets and makes fools of diviners . . ." (Isaiah 44:24, 25).

God has no patience with our desire to seek out other avenues of information concerning His plan. How *can* we please Him while we seek to discover what He has chosen to keep veiled?

What are the doubtful practices we need to beware of? How have even well-meaning Christians fallen into this trap set by our souls' enemy?

16
Good News According to the Zodiac

At the end of the turbulent 1960s, a new theme was emerging from the hippie movement. We all heard the message through a snappy popular song, "The Age of Aquarius," by the popular band the Fifth Dimension.

The song signaled what astrologers and occultists had been talking about for a long time. The Age of Aquarius was coming—in 1982 the sun moved into the sixth constellation of the zodiac, called Aquarius. For a long time many considered this a key sign and perhaps a symbol of the stars guiding mankind to a new unity—maybe even a new world order.

Psychologist Carl Jung—himself an avid occult practitioner—looked forward to the Age of Aquarius. The Age of Pisces, the Christian era, would yield to Aquarius, the era of the Holy Spirit, he said. It would bring in a utopian age—a time of peace, understanding and love ruled over by the planet Uranus, which represents sudden changes, he added.[1] Perhaps sparked by this widespread acceptance of the occult, the fastest growing modern religious movement in America—the New Age movement—kicked into high gear in 1982.

Make no mistake about it. Astrology and occultism are intertwined, as they always have been from ancient days. According to *The Facts on Astrology,* by John Ankerberg and John Weldon, "The very practice of astrology is a foundational occult art and . . . the practitioners [astrologers] open themselves up to becoming involved in other occult practices."[2] They point out that astrology is related to the occult in "four major ways":

> First, astrology itself is defined by Webster's Dictionary as an occult art. As such it employs occult practices such as divination. Divination may be defined as "the art of obtaining secret or illegitimate knowledge of the future by methods unsanctioned by and at variance with the holiness of God" and which involve contact with evil spirits. Secondly, astrology appears to work best when the astrologer himself is psychically sensitive, what most astrologers would term "intuitive." Thirdly, prolonged use of astrology often leads to the development of psychic abilities. Fourthly, due to its history and very nature, astrology often becomes the introductory course to a wider spectrum of occult practices.[3]

Yet despite its direct connection with occultism, prominent soothsayers of the Second Advent teach astrology to the church, even declaring that by entering the Age of Aquarius, the stars may be signaling the great tribulation, followed by the Second Coming of Jesus Christ. Combining the "message" of the stars and the testimony of the Bible, David Webber and Noah Hutchings of the Southwest Radio Church saw the coming of the Aquarian age as the end of the Dispensation of Grace and the beginning of the millennium.[4]

Colin Deal also claimed astrology had something to do with Christ's birth and now His return, which he said would happen "by 1988." He relied upon 1976 and 1977 newspaper and magazine articles suggesting that the 1982 conjunction of Jupiter and Saturn and the 1986 reappearance of Halley's comet were similar to astrological signs around 7 B.C., the approximate time of Christ's birth. (Halley's comet was thought to have appeared two years earlier, at 9 B.C.) One article stated: "As 1982 approaches, the planets will be moving into the sign of Aquarius. This sign is pictured as 'The Water Bringer.' " It goes on to say that by combining the meanings of the names of three stars found in Aquarius, and with the water bringer meaning Jesus Christ, it means that Christ "left, but returned to pour out waters of blessings upon a people redeemed for the earth."[5]

To that Deal adds: "Yes . . . the signs of the heavens are declaring for the first time in 2,000 years that God's Son is about to be revealed!"[6] However, even if you use the meanings assigned to the stars by the proponents of "Christian astrology" or "glory in the stars" theory, the article Deal quoted is in error. The names of the three brightest stars in that constellation *do not* have any relevant meaning at all.[7]

Webber and Hutchings, at the Southwest Radio Church, have laid out their "Christian astrology" theory in greater detail. In *Apocalyptic Signs in the Heavens*, they speculated on a conjunction of planets before Moses' birth.[8] Citing ancient historians, they supposed that Egyptian astrologers foresaw the prophet's birth and that this led to the killing of the Israelite infants.[9]

However, their speculations about the conjunction being a reason behind pharaoh's killing the male children shoots wide of the biblical record. Exodus 1:6–22 states that because of a population explosion by the Israelites ". . . the land was filled with them" (Exodus 1:7), and the king of Egypt feared the Jews might become more numerous than the Egyptians and eventually "join our enemies, fight against us and leave the country" (Exodus 1:10). That is the *only* biblical record of his reasons for ordering the deaths of the children.

Later Webber and Hutchings suggested that Cyrus, the king of Persia, commissioned the Jews to rebuild their temple on the basis of astrological revelation. They favorably compared Zoroastrianism, the religion of Persia, to Judaism, because it taught that a messiah would come.[10] They even saw the Persian religion as something that developed from the worship of God.[11]

But to imply that Cyrus, king of Persia, was motivated by the heathen art of astrology to rebuild God's temple comes close to blasphemy, especially when the Bible says that the Lord God *Himself* motivated the king, whom God called His anointed in Isaiah 45:1. Ezra chronicled it:

> In the first year of Cyrus king of Persia, in order to fulfill the word of the Lord spoken by Jeremiah, the Lord moved the heart of Cyrus king of Persia to make a proclamation throughout his realm and to put it in writing . . . "The Lord, the God of heaven . . . has appointed me to build a temple for him at Jerusalem. . . ."
>
> Ezra 1:1, 2

The same can be said for Webber and Hutchings's comparing Judaism to Zoroastrianism. Although some have compared a few of the sayings of Jesus to Zoroaster, the foundations of the two religions are diametrically different. "Most Christians believe in three Persons in the Godhead: Father, Son, and Holy Spirit," writes Marcus Bach in his book, *Major Religions of the World*. "Zoroastrians, however, believe there are *seven* persons in the Godhead."[12]

The Southwest Radio Church duo also took Deal's thoughts on Christ's birth occurring during the conjunctions of Saturn and Jupiter a step farther. Quoting *The Gospel in the Stars*, by Joseph A. Seiss—which is one of the leading Christian astrology books—they claim that Jupiter and Saturn conjuncted three times during the year of Christ's birth. Webber and Hutchings then suggested the three conjunctions mean the three Persons of the Godhead.[13]

The astrological signs have continued to this century, they wrote. They stated that in 1917, along with the signing of the Balfour Declaration, which recognized the land of Palestine as the national homeland of the Jews, "there were four total eclipses of the sun, and three eclipses of the moon." In 1918, when the World Zionist Organization endorsed the document, "a new star appeared in the heavens . . . it shone brightly for 40 days. Forty is the Jewish number of testing."[14]

Seeing Redemption in the Stars

What is the theory behind "glory in the stars" theology? According to Albert Dager, a Christian who runs the Washington-state-based Media Spotlight, it's the belief that "the Zodiac was originally designed by God as a witness of His plan of redemption, and was later corrupted to occult science into an instrument of divination (the predicting of the future and/or the determining of personality traits based on the positions of the heavenly bodies)."[15]

Colin Deal, J. R. Church, David Webber, Noah Hutchings and other like-minded prophecy teachers all cite the work of E. W. Bullinger (1837–1913). Bullinger, an Anglican clergyman and descendant of Swiss Reformer J. Heinrich Bullinger, partly edited *The Companion Bible.* He was also one of the most controversial theologians in recent centuries, because he taught a type of Christian astrology, numerology, and pyramidology.

Dager and others knowledgeable about this starry theology say the earliest traceable work in the field was done by Florence Rolleston of Keswick, England. She devoted over fifty years of her life to "the compilation of a massive series of notes which was published under the title *Mazzaroth—The Constellations* in 1863, when she was in her 80's," writes William D. Banks, a proponent of "Christian astrology."[16] In 1884 her concepts, which included the listings of ancient astronomical facts, significance, and the names of a hundred or more stars, gained more acceptance with the release of *The Gospel in the Stars,* by Joseph A. Seiss. But Bullinger's book, *The Witness of the Stars,* which came out in 1893, took Miss Rolleston's theories even further, because he stated that for the stars' "interpretation I am alone responsible."[17]

From there Bullinger incorporated astrology into other areas of his theology. In *The Companion Bible,* partly edited by Bullinger, he stated that the words of Scripture parallel the words written in the heavens and preserved by the zodiac. Bullinger also added that all the verbs in the second half of Psalm 19 are of an astronomical nature. In a work often cited by today's prophecy teachers, *Number in Scripture,* Bullinger fused Bible numerology with the zodiac.

But Dager said all theories such as Bullinger's are based on "conjecture. In so doing they have—with all good intention, I'm sure, melded God's truth with pagan myth, traceable no further back than Babylon."[18] There is simply no record existing that God originally created the zodiac signs as Christian symbols, which were later perverted by the occult and modern astrologers, to reveal His eternal plan. Writes Dager:

> Though Bullinger's theory is brilliantly stated, pointing out the Scripture's references to certain of the stars and constellations by their astrological names, the basis for his argument is found wanting. Wrote Bullinger, "After the Revelation came to be written down in the Scriptures, there was not the same need for the preservation of the Heavenly Volume. And after the nations had lost the original meaning of the pictures, they invented a meaning out of the vain imagination of the thoughts of their hearts." . . . [But] the fact is that the pagan interpretations of the Zodiac are the only ones of which any legitimate records exist, and they predate the Gospels by at least two thousand years.[19]

Bullinger also claimed to have found scriptural justification for his "glory in the stars" theory. He claimed Paul was referring to the zodiac in Romans 1:19, 20:[20] "Since what may be known about God is plain to them, because God has made it plain to them. For since the creation of the world God's invisible qualities—his eternal power and divine nature—have been clearly seen, being understood from what has been made, so that men are without excuse." He also used Romans 10:18, which "is similar to Psalm 19:1–6 which refers to the heavens declaring the glory of God," wrote Dager.[21]

Bullinger also misapplied Scriptures dealing with the tower of Babel, in an apparent attempt to refute traditional charges that God scattered humanity so they couldn't complete the tower. Some commentaries have taught that the tower was an astrological attempt to reach into the heavens for more occult meanings. Bullinger, ignoring the biblical record, said that the sin was not in building the tower; it was in failing to disperse over the earth.[22]

Today's Signs?

As their theological father Bullinger did, today's soothsayers of the Second Advent distort the Scriptures to make them appear to affirm a type of astrology.

Colin Deal inserted "inscribe as a writer" in the middle of Psalm 19:1, 2 to imply it was talking about astrology: "What, then, was the true meaning of (the verse) . . . 'the heavens declare (inscribe as a writer) the glory of God . . .'?" He also quotes Job 38:32, "Can you bring forth the constellations in their seasons. . . ?" and Genesis 1:14, "And God said, 'Let there be lights in the expanse of the sky to separate the day from the night, and let them serve as signs to mark seasons and days and years,' " as proof of the astrological principle.[23]

Deal also says that Jesus claimed there would be *astrological* signs that would precede His Second Coming. His proof text? Luke 21:25: "There will be signs in the sun, moon and stars. . . ."[24] But Deal—and Webber and Hutchings, who used the same verse[25]—conveniently failed to mention that in parallel texts in both Matthew 24:29 and Mark 13:24, 25, Jesus explained what he meant. He said that after incredible distress on the earth, "the sun will be darkened, and the moon will not give its light; the stars will fall from the sky, and the heavenly bodies will be shaken." Even more telling, Deal does not mention the same description of the signs of the end of time mentioned in Isaiah 13:10; 34:4; Ezekiel 32:7; Joel 2:10, 31; Zephaniah 1:15; and Revelation 6:12, 13; 8:12.

Using Psalm 19 to justify astrology is out of line; the meaning is clear. Every time we go out on a quiet, clear, and dark night in the countryside and look up, it is obvious that the "heavens declare the glory of God." What a breathtaking sight, particularly when one is reminded that God made all the stars! Genesis 1:14 as proof for astrology is no better; it simply states that God made the stars and sun. Through them we could know the seasons, days and years.

Webber and Hutchings also use Psalm 19:1, 2 and Job 38 to justify their brand of astrology. But they go further, much, much further. They claim—without documenting it—that "Job and the Psalms spoke of them [the stars] as authentic outlines of God's revelation."[26] They also suggest that Jesus was referring to astrology affirming His arrival in Matthew 16:3:[27] ". . . You know how to interpret the appearance of the sky, but you cannot interpret the signs of the times." It's interesting, again, to note that Webber and Hutchings ignored the first part of the verse and the preceding one in which Jesus tells us that the appearance of the sky has to do with the "weather," not with the stars.

Confusion in the Stars?

Of course all the while Webber, Hutchings, and Deal practice their brand of heavenly astrology, they denounce other forms of the practice. Deal said: "Demonic astrology, found abundantly in newspapers and magazines, is strictly forbidden in God's word (Isaiah 47:12–14)."[28] Southwest has consistently condemned known psychics such as Jeane Dixon, because they rely on astrology.

It's interesting that in 1978 Webber and Hutchings quoted Nostradamus, a sixteenth-century "prophet," positively to imply that our present pope, John Paul II, would be history's last one.[29] (Nostradamus allegedly saw the end of the world around the year 2000). But two years later Southwest's the *Gospel Truth* ran an anonymous article *condemning* Nostradamus's prophecies, because they learned "he used astrology to prophesy, which God condemns."[30] The article didn't mention that Nostradamus practiced other forms of the occult (including out-of-body trances) and was persecuted by French and church officials for doing so.[31]

Quoting Dixon *favorably* was Edgar Whisenant. In reason 65 in his *88 Reasons Why the Rapture Will Be in 1988*, he wrote that Dixon—"today's famous psychic"—foresaw the birth of a future world leader on February 5, 1962. In reason 66 Whisenant said that this leader born on that date is "our Antichrist of the end-time." And Whisenant isn't the only prophecy teacher proclaiming that. R. Henry Hall of Las Vegas believes it,[32] along with a ministry in Cleburne, Texas, called "The Eschatology Hour," which produced an audiotape on the subject.

What Do These Revelations Mean?

As Ankerberg and Weldon point out, "Just as oil and water do not mix, the Bible and astrology are utterly irreconcilable. . . . As both a philosophy and practice, astrology rejects the truth concerning the living God and instead leads people to dead objects, the stars and planets."[33]

Therefore, today's prophecy teachers ought to stop all speculation about the meaning of stars and stop looking for conjunctions and objects in space to tell us about future events such as the great tribulation and the Second Coming of Christ. Astrology is a weapon in the arsenal of Satan, one he tries to use against the church in these last days. There is simply no evidence to suggest that in ancient times God revealed Himself and His plan in the zodiac. Moreover I see little difference between astrology columns in the daily newspaper and astrological speculations that predict end-time events.

Besides, through His Son, Jesus, we have all we need to know about the Second Advent. Hebrews 1:2 states: ". . . in these last days he has spoken to us by his Son, whom he appointed heir of all things, and through whom he made the universe" (including the stars).

Second, prophecy teachers—or any Christian—who justifies the use of any form of astrology, should stop ignoring the heavy weight of Scripture that condemns the practice in *any* form and stop taking God's Word out of context in an attempt to affirm it. I would admonish the prophecy teachers mentioned in this chapter to reread the Scripture verses ("the whole counsel of God") concerning astrology. God says the counsel of astrologers is worthless, and it won't even save the astrologers (*see* Deuteronomy 4:19; 17:1–5; 18:9–11; 2 Kings 17:16, 17; 23:5; Jeremiah 8:2; 19:13; Ezekiel 8:16; Amos 5:26, 27;[34] *see also* Isaiah 47:13, 14, already referred to by Deal).

As Ankerberg and Weldon point out: "The Bible teaches that astrology is not only a futile (worthless) activity, but an activity so bad that its very presence indicates God's judgment has already occurred (Acts 7:42–43)."[35] It is also occult, and as we'll soon see, it has led to some prophecy teachers' embracing other occult practices such as pyramidology and numerology.

17
Hidden Dangers of the Cabala

Did God implant hidden prophecies in the Psalms, designed for earth's last generation to decipher?

That's the concept advanced by J. R. Church in his well-written book, *Hidden Prophecies in the Psalms*. It immediately grabbed the attention of many other prophecy teachers as the words *Major Discovery* were written in bold letters on the cover of the book. It has sold well, too. According to Church's January, 1989, newsletter, 110,000 copies went in the first eighteen months—not bad for a self-published book, or for any Christian book, for that matter.

Although Church had been a prophecy teacher for some time before the book was published and had hosted a weekly syndicated television program, "Prophecy in the News," in cities across America, *Hidden Prophecies* thrust him more solidly into the limelight. Many other teachers, such as Edgar Whisenant, Charles Taylor, and Henry Kreysler, have cited Church's work as he has participated in many prophecy conferences and speaking engagements. Church's organization, Prophecy Publications, also publishes a monthly newsletter called *Prophecy in the News*.

Church's theory about the Psalms is relatively easy. One day his research assistant, Patricia Berry, asked him to turn to Psalm 48 and read verses 4–6. Then she asked, "Doesn't that sound like the United Nations giving birth to the state of Israel [in 1948]?" Next she directed him to Psalm 17 and claimed that it sounded "like a description of the British general, Allenby, taking Jerusalem in 1917."[1]

Church went on to find comparisons between the first three Psalms and the first three years of the 1900s. Because the book of Psalms is the nineteenth book of the Old Testament, he began to figure that it had to describe this century.[2] Therefore the 400-page book is in many ways an interesting history lesson as Church weaves in many accurate details about the trials the Jews have faced in the twentieth century.

As Church went further in his research, he wondered about the future Psalms—the ones from 86 to 100. Did they tell God's plans in advance from 1986 to 2000? What about Psalms 100 to 150? Did they also speak of the future? Yes! Church wrote. But this also posed a dilemma for him. He thought he saw the rapture of the church, the tribulation, the Antichrist, and the Second Coming of Christ just ahead. Dare he publish his findings?

"It is with some degree of reluctance, then, that I even approach the subject for fear of being labeled as a date setter," he wrote, explaining his mental processes at the time. Though he in no way wanted to wear this label, he felt he would be remiss in his calling if he failed to publish it.[3]

Church solved his dilemma: He published his findings, which included projected dates future events would probably occur, then sprinkled them with disclaimers, sometimes shifting the interpretations to other sources. (Church has always stated his thesis is a theory.) In implying that 1988 might see the beginning of the tribulation and the rapture, he stated that he's not the one suggesting it; the Bible seems to imply it:

> I can go no further than to say that the later Psalms seem to set a TREND for those events which the Bible's prophets say will someday come to pass.

> It was not I who put a reference to the resurrection [rapture] in Psalm 88:10, nor would I dare to suggest that the resurrection must occur in 1988.[4]

Church takes strong exception to anyone implying that he is a date setter. But the fact remains that he *has* chosen years for a number of end-time events, sprinkled with vague disclaimers, and then has shown us why—in detail in many cases—the Psalms seem to point to these dates. He has, in fact, described the projected 1988-1994 tribulation in great detail in his book on pages 245–282, again sprinkled with disclaimers.

He then suggests a 1988 rapture *six times* in his chapter on Psalm 88;[5] suggests the Antichrist will set a trap for the Jewish people perhaps (but not necessarily) as early as 1988;[6] implies that the two witnesses, identified as Elijah and Moses, referred to in Revelation 11 might appear in 1989–1990;[7] talks about the Antichrist committing the "abomination of desolation" on the Temple Mount in Jerusalem in Psalm 91 (while simultaneously 144,000 Jews flee to Petra); records the "dreadful Battle of Armageddon" in Psalm 94; and notes that the world "rejoices over the appearance of Christ to save the day" in Psalm 95.[8]

"Unveiling" the Signs

For those who do not believe there are prophecies in the Psalms, Church says look again. He says Jesus referred to them in Luke 24:44. Later Church claimed the first part of the verse, which speaks of the fulfillment of the law of Moses and the prophets, was fulfilled in the first century, but the last part of His statement, which speaks of prophecies in the Psalms, concerning Him, "describes the end of the era. . . . It is as if God took the prophecies in the Psalms, put them on the shelf in His closet of secret things and closed the door until the last generation."[9]

J. R. Church claims he may have been the man to unveil many of these secret things.

Most proficient Bible students know there *are* prophecies

in the Psalms, many of which have been well-defined for centuries. J. R. Church is also correct that some of the prophecies do indicate the soon coming of the Lord. For example, it's hard to get around Psalm 102:16: "For the Lord will rebuild Zion and appear in his glory." Zion, or Israel, has been rebuilt. The Jews are back in their homeland. Now we're waiting for the Lord to return.

Nowhere in Luke 24:44 did Jesus imply the Psalms were veiled. The context of the verse also clearly shows that Jesus was telling His disciples about the prophecies in the Psalms that already had been fulfilled about Him *in the past*. Let's go back to the passage. The background of the passage is that after Christ's resurrection He appeared to the disciples out of nowhere and frightened them. Then he explained to them in detail that the prophecies had to do with His life on earth, His death and resurrection. "Then he opened their minds so they could understand the Scriptures. He told them, 'This is what is written: The Christ will suffer and rise from the dead on the third day' " (Luke 24:45, 46).

There are *many* prophecies in the Psalms about Jesus' first coming.

Psalm 16:10 refers to His resurrection.
Psalm 22 refers to His crucifixion in graphic terms.
Psalm 31:5 contains Jesus' last words on the cross.
Psalm 34:20 prophesies that none of Christ's bones would be broken.
Psalm 41:9 implies His betrayal by Judas.
Psalm 69:9–21 contains two prophecies, including one that He would be given vinegar for His thirst, which happened at His crucifixion.
Psalm 118:22 echoes Christ's words to the Pharisees that the stone the builders rejected will be the capstone.

But Church's hidden prophecies are not like these; they are unique and radically different. More troublesome is that Church has developed methods of discerning the "hidden" prophecies that are not even hinted at in the Word of God.

In short, Church has developed a private interpretation of prophecy.

That means red flags should go up. Remember the Apostle Peter's warning as he instructed the early church that they should pay close attention to the word of the prophets: "Above all, you must understand that no prophecy of Scripture came about by the prophet's own [some versions read *private*] interpretation. For prophecy never had its origin in the will of man, but men spoke from God as they were carried along by the Holy Spirit" (2 Peter 1:20, 21).

How do we know that Church's "hidden prophecies" aren't his private interpretation and therefore not from God at all?

Let's look at some of Church's hidden prophecies in the Psalms.

Though commentators do not say so, Church believes Psalm 48 "clearly" prophesies the revival of national Israel.[10] You might recall that this Psalm is the one that led Church on his quest to find other hidden prophecies. He cites verses 4–6 (KJV) as the key: "For, lo, the kings were assembled, they passed by together. They saw it, and so they marvelled; they were troubled, and hasted away. Fear took hold upon them there, and pain, as of a woman in travail."[11]

Now stop. Read the verses again. Do they "clearly" show the creation of Israel? I don't think so. But Church decodes them: "The assembled *kings* could imply a group of representatives from various governments and the *woman in travail*, the rebirth of the state of Israel."[12]

Elsewhere Church describes the phase the "snare of the fowler" in the Psalms as referring to the "Antichrist." In Psalm 80 Church describes "the vine out of Egypt" as Anwar Sadat.[13] In Psalm 17 the phrase "Keep me as the apple of the eye, hide me under the shadow of thy wings," (v. 8 KJV) is said to mean General Allenby ordering airplanes to fly over Jerusalem.[14] There are many other examples, but the point is that he uses a subjective system.

His system is also riddled with inconsistencies. In Psalm 94, which he claims "describes the devastation to be wrought at Armageddon," the term " '*shew thyself*' . . . [v. 1 KJV] implies a prophetic prayer for Christ to appear on the day of His vengeance." In Psalm 95 He has come. But Psalm 80:1 also contains the same term—"shew thyself"—and Church ignored it.

With his suggested 1988–1994 tribulation scenario already failing, Church has begun to backpedal. He denies implying a 1988 rapture, and now he denies that he implied that the two witnesses (Moses and Elijah) were scheduled to appear in 1989 or 1990. In an article he wrote in January, 1989, for his newsletter, Church said nothing about the possibility of Elijah and Moses coming in his "prophetic prospects" for 1989. Instead he mentioned the Soviet Union initiating a sneak attack against the United States and that possibly Egypt would be involved in a "coming war."[15]

(In a book published in the summer of 1989 by the Southwest Radio Church, Church claimed "Psalms 88 describes the Palestinian unrest in the occupied territories."[16] The trouble is, Church never mentioned the coming Palestinian unrest that was so much in the news during 1988 in *Hidden Prophecies*.)

In the chapter on Psalm 89 in *Hidden Prophecies,* he spoke of other possibilities for 1989: "Psalm 89 and 90 seem to present the messages of two future witnesses, Elijah and Moses, who will come to lead the 144,000 during the first half of the Tribulation Period. Though we do not have the name of Elijah in Psalm 89, the message appears to be the kind Elijah would give to the Jews."[17] Five more times in the chapter Church refers to the future Elijah's message.

Did Church hint at a 1988 rapture? I believe he did, because he seems to say that in Psalm 88 Christians are no longer on earth.[18]

The Source of These Interpretations

Perhaps our more serious concerns are that Church may have used occult means to come up with some of his interpretations. This was implied by cult expert Dean Halverson in the Fall, 1988, issue of the *Christian Research Journal*, when he stated that Edgar Whisenant engaged in "occult numerology" in coming up with one of his "88 Reasons" why the rapture would occur in 1988.[19]

Halverson cited Whisenant's reason 61 as the example, and that's one in which Whisenant quotes Church. Whisenant wrote that when Church visited an Orthodox rabbi, the meaning of the Hebrew year 5749 (which is from Rosh Hashanah, 1988, to Rosh Hashanah, 1989) the rabbi told him it spells *Shemittah*, the word for "sabbatical year."[20] Reason 62 also contains similar reasoning—attributing meanings to numbers—by Church, though Halverson did not cite it.

Does attributing meanings to numbers mean someone was dabbling in the occult? I studied what occult numerology really was. The result is an increased concern that Church has—perhaps unknowingly—dabbled in the practice.

Although there are different types of occult numerology systems, one of the most frequently used forms is associated with the Jewish Cabala, according to occult experts. The Cabala is a Jewish oral tradition of hidden wisdom. No one really knows where it came from. It is a type of mysticism that's separate from Jewish doctrinal orthodoxy.[21] While not all of the Cabala is associated with the occult, some of it definitely is.

John Warwick Montgomery, a renowned Christian apologist, wrote that the Cabala employs three methods to interpret the Bible by numbers: Gematria, Notarikon, and Themurah.[22] Montgomery noted:

> These methods were used for two prime purposes: first and foremost, to derive from the Scriptures a hidden, occult meaning; second, to validate the Scriptures as literally inspired of God by showing the remarkable numerical relationships which presumably existed in them.[23]

It can be demonstrated that Church uses two of the three (Gematria and Notarikon) Cabalistic methods of interpreting the Bible throughout *Hidden Prophecies*. Since the examples are so numerous we'll only look at several of them.

Gematria is the process of taking the numerical values of words and creating equivalences for them. One way it is employed is by adding "the values of the *names* of the letters (the first letter of the Hebrew alphabet, *aleph* = 111)."[24] Compare that to J. R. Church's chapter on Psalms 88. When he asked a Jewish friend to tell him what the Hebrew number would be for the phonetic word *eighty-eight*, his answer was *pach*. Wrote Church, "I asked him, 'What does it mean?' and he replied, 'It is how you say a trap—like a pit.' " From that conversation, Church figured out the "hidden prophecy": "This antichrist will lay a trap through which he will plan the genocide of the Jews. In a manner similar to that of Adolf Hitler, he will deceive the whole world."[25]

Montgomery says Notarikon is an "acrostic system." Quoting another source, he noted that it works by taking first or final letters of the words of a phrase, joining them together to form a word "which was then given occult significance."[26] Try Church's analysis of Psalm 92 on for size:

> Psalm 92 continues with an assessment of the antichrist, a *brutish man* and a description of the approaching armies for the Battle of Armageddon. The number 92 is made up of two Hebrew letters "tzade" and "beth." They make up the word "tsawb" with three possible meanings: 1) "a litter, a covered and curtained couch provided with shafts and used for carrying a single passenger." Here is a perfect description of the triumphal entry of the antichrist onto the Temple Mount. 2) "To establish, a canopy (as a fixture)." The antichrist will enter the Sanctuary on the Temple Mount and offer himself as the Messiah of Israel. 3) "A species of lizard." Could this allude to the dragon of Revelation? There is yet another word derived from

> the number 92. If we add an additional "Aleph" it becomes "Tsawba" meaning "to muster soldiers for war." The war clouds of Armageddon appear to be brewing.[27]

Church didn't say in the book how he found this method of interpretation leading to his discoveries in the Psalms. He does quote various rabbis, Jewish friends, and some books pertaining to the history of the Jewish people. Perhaps he picked up some Cabalistic influence there. But he very clearly agreed with many of the ideas on Bible numerics from none other than the theologian of the soothsayers, E. W. Bullinger. He quotes Bullinger's numbering techniques throughout his book.

Did Bullinger's numerology techniques differ from the occult ones used in the Cabala? No, says Montgomery, who bemoaned the fact that "a reputable American evangelical publisher" has done two printings of Bullinger's *Number in Scripture*, in the 1960s, without revisions "or even a new preface to warn readers of its questionable arguments."[28]

Montgomery rejected Cabalistic interpretations of Scripture for three reasons:

1. There is no justification in Scripture for Hebrew being the sacred language.
2. The Scriptures never advocate interpreting Scripture that way. (Could you imagine Christ asking His disciples to add numerical values of words together in order to find a hidden meaning?)
3. It is not capable of revealing truth due to the many possible—and contradictory—meanings that can be gleaned from such methods.

The "hidden prophecies" theory should be rejected as unbiblical. It has already proven to be inaccurate and inconsistent. It also is a "private interpretation" of prophecy, such as Peter warned against. It definitely goes "beyond what is written" (1 Corinthians 4:6) in God's Word.

Is There Good News in Bible Numerics?

J. R. Church is not the only one using occult numbering techniques to discern prophecy. Some such as David Webber, Noah Hutchings, and others dabble in numerics in the best tradition of E. W. Bullinger.

But is there any basis for the idea that there is a "scriptural" (nonoccult) numerics system in the Bible that can benefit the church? I don't think so. First, although some have worked out detailed Bible-numerics systems, they are all inconsistent. Almost every "workable" numbering scheme requires incredible ingenuity to sustain it.[29] Both Montgomery and Oswald Allis, the author of the 1944 Moody Press book, *Bible Numerics,* suggested that with enough ingenuity one could mathematically prove the divine nature of any printed text, even the daily newspaper or the United States Constitution.

Second, the Bible was never intended to prove mathematical formulas. Noted Allis:

> . . . The Bible is not a book for mathematical experts to exercise their ingenuity on. There is not a scintilla of real evidence to show that the writers of the Bible were conscious of writing "numerically," or were aware that back of their words there is a hidden numeric cryptogram of such importance than men are justified in devoting their lives to the discovery and elucidation of its mysteries. . . . Bible Numerics has a certain fascination. But its wizardry reminds us of the obfuscating *abracadabra* of alchemist and astrologer; it is not marked by the simplicity of the Gospel.[30]

Allis made some final observations about it: It's ". . . a tremendous waste of time and effort. . . . A man who rests his faith in the inerrancy of the Bible on Bible Numerics is trusting in a broken reed, which if he leans on it will go into his hand and pierce it."[31]

18
Stone Soothsayers

It was reminiscent of a scene from the movie *Indiana Jones and the Temple of Doom*.

Except, for me, it was real.

I was at the Great Pyramid at Giza, Egypt, the only one of the seven wonders of the ancient world still standing. I was about to go inside the monstrous structure, to the very belly, called the King's Chamber.

I was part of a Temple University study tour to Israel and Egypt that summer, and I still remember the excitement of just being there. Soon after we climbed inside the small door carved into the pyramid's exterior and worked our way along a dark, narrow passageway, sloping upward, I thought I detected a muffled sound reverberating in the cavernlike tunnel. We worked ahead, groping upward in the dank passageway that sloped upward at an even steeper angle. In minutes the passageway narrowed, and the ceiling squeezed downward to a mere four feet high, forcing us on our hands and knees to continue the thirty-minute climb. But as we continued on I knew I was hearing something otherworldly, something mysterious, making an already eerie atmosphere even more forboding. HUMMM! HUMMM! HUMMM! HUMMM! It sounded like a bizarre, timed, rhythmic tone that resonated off the stones around us. The farther we went, the louder it got.

As we got to the Grand Gallery, a part of the passageway where the tunnel widens and opens to reveal a high ceiling, the noise became deafening. It clouded our thinking as we observed light ahead of us, revealing that the passageway emptied into a room.

Ducking under a stone, we found ourselves at the heart of the pyramid, inside the King's Chamber, which Egyptologists say was the burial vault of Cheops, one of ancient Egypt's greatest pharaohs and the one credited with building the pyramid. Now it became clear what the noise was, too. Holding hands in a circle around the stone burial crypt were about twelve young adults—members of an American cult, all in an ecstatic, glassy-eyed trance—calling on the powers of the ancient Egyptian gods, as one of them was lying in the crypt.

There wasn't much else in the King's Chamber. Our little group stayed there for a while and observed the strange happenings. The cultists were so deep into their ceremony that they didn't know we were there. They remained long after we left; we could hear them chanting the same rhythmic stanzas as we exited.

The Attraction of Pyramids

It's not surprising that the Rosicrucian cult was in the heart of the pyramid that day. The pyramids have long been an object of fascination for many mystical and occult groups. I later found out that the Rosicrucians are obsessed with ancient Egyptian religion, and they conduct pilgrimages to the King's Chamber, which they call the Hall of Illumination, a place of secret initiation.

The pyramids are also big with some New Age groups and channelers. J. Z. Knight, the Seattle-area guru to Shirley MacLaine, who claims to channel a 35,000-year-old warrior from Atlantis, named Ramtha, said she was able to create a "petrified cockroach" by placing a small pyramid over it. Later when she held a polka-dotted pyramid to her brain, an entity appeared to her in her kitchen, saying, "I am Ramtha, the enlightened one. I have come to help you over the ditch. I have come to teach you to be a light unto the world."[1]

Many satanists are into pyramids, too. The San Francisco based Temple of Set, which believes the Christian church has twisted the truth away from the "fact" that Satan is the true creator of the universe, sees prophetic significance in the Great Pyramid and claims there is magic and great wisdom in ancient Egyptian occult witchcraft. Other satanists believe there's power in the drawn image of a pyramid. They call it the "triangle" or "power cone." A drawing of a pyramid is placed on the ground during satanic rituals to confine the demonic forces conjured up.[2]

Not surprisingly the fascination has overflowed to other sects, including some that claim an affinity to biblical Christianity. In 1931 the Deseret News Publishing Company, the official publisher of the Mormon Church, printed *Our Bible in Stone: The Great Pyramid of Gizeh*. The book used nearly 150 pages of computations, adding Matthew to Daniel, minus the square root of one of the Mormons' guiding books (*Doctrines and Covenants*), multiplied by the dimensions of the Great Pyramid. The conclusion was that the date of "A.D. 1940 was found . . . to be the extreme limit for the Second Coming of Christ."[3]

But don't laugh too hard yet. Some otherwise orthodox Christians are into it, too.

Some of them are today's prophecy teachers, who use the Great Pyramid as a soothsaying device to calculate end-time events. What's interesting about this is that Bible pyramidology is the older cousin by about two decades of so-called "Christian astrology." In fact two of the theological proponents of the stars theory—E. W. Bullinger and Joseph Seiss—also became champions of the pyramid or "Bible in stone" theory.

Bullinger and Seiss and others who came after them were aware of various astronomical aspects of the Great Pyramid. Bullinger was impressed with an astrological fact—it requires 25,826 years for the sun to make its journey through the twelve signs of the zodiac, and somehow the pyramid and the nearby sphinx reflected that. The base of the pyramid, measuring in at 25,826 inches long, also reflected that, according to pyramidologists. Could an inch reflect a year? (Question: Why an inch, instead of a unit from the metric system that most of the world uses?) Also intriguing was that the Descending Passage of the Great Pyramid in Giza seemed to have pointed to the North Star (also called the Dragon Star) at 2200 B.C., which was roughly the time period of its construction.

From these facts and others the early pyramidologists jumped to an incredible conclusion: God either personally built the pyramid or ordered it built to His specifications to serve as a written record—a Bible in stone—of His plans for the world.

Today's prophecy teachers have picked up a lot of their ideas from Bullinger, Seiss, and a handful of others. They also cite many other reasons for believing the Great Pyramid is God's Bible in stone. Let's let David Webber and Noah Hutchings explain it in their own words:

> God is called the "Master Builder," and man can only imitate the handiwork of His perfect creations. The fact that the Great Pyramid is the most perfect building to be erected on earth indicates a divine origin.[4]

> That the Great Pyramid of Giza, the original pyramid, was built by a higher intelligence and constructed within a pattern which sets forth God's eternal plan (and) purpose for the Earth, is beyond question.[5]

In an April 19, 1989, interview with David Webber, he said that despite many associations of pyramidology with the occult, that doesn't mean the Great Pyramid is not founded on truth. "I believe it is God's Bible in stone,"

Webber said. "Because we don't perfectly understand it is no reason to throw it out. I realize pyramidology is big in the occult and the New Age movement, but the devil's a great imitator."

Christian Pyramidology?

"Isaiah said it [the Great Pyramid] would be for a sign in that day (last day)," wrote Colin Deal. "It not only reveals knowledge of the birth, death, burial and resurrection of our Lord; but prophetic timetables based on measurements in the Great Pyramid have been discovered which relate to the Twentieth Century."[6]

But not all prophecy teachers mentioned in this book agree on the matter. Doug Clark said that he "went to Cairo many times with a measuring tape" to try to run his own tests on the pyramid. The results were less than conclusive, he mused. "It's so confusing, it's ridiculous," said Clark. "So I think it's a myth."[7]

Another prophecy teacher, Reginald Dunlop, writing in the mid-1970s, wound up with egg on his face when he asserted the pyramid revealed a *definite date of 1979* for the start of the millennium, and there "is no longer any room for anybody's opinions."[8]

Moving forward to 1988, Edgar Whisenant, in his *88 Reasons,* affirmed that the pyramid had "prophetic" significance in a sense. It's the devil's prophecy in stone, he wrote. "The main shaft of the Great Pyramid of Giza was pointing directly at the star Draconis in the heavens when the Pyramid was built. The star Draconis stands for Satan "*. . . it is of Satan, and it is a record of an inch to the year except in the King's chamber where it is a foot to the year of all the evil things Satan was going to put on man throughout his history.*"[9]

Whisenant's comments about the pyramid drew an angry response from the Southwest Radio Church. So much so that Hutchings commissioned California pyramid expert Ralph Lyman to critique Whisenant's 1988 rapture theory. The result was a twenty-six-page booklet that concluded that Whisenant was off on many of his calculations. Whisenant was *really off* with his ideas on the Great Pyramid, Lyman asserted. The last six pages of the book is a diatribe against Whisenant's devil-pyramid theory. "Jesus Christ endorsed the Pyramid, referring to Himself as the chief cornerstone rejected by the builders," Lyman proclaimed. "The Great Pyramid is the only pyramid with a missing capstone."[10]

These last examples of confusion, contradicting opinions, and outright date-setting errors using Great Pyramid theories are typical. In fact, the history of Christian pyramidology is so tenuous, so filled with date-setting errors that I'm surprised any ministries are still using it to "prove" anything. Unfortunately, pyramidology is making a strong comeback from the 1920s and 1930s, when it fell into disrepute after "prophecies" of the end supposedly gleaned from the wonder in Giza failed to materialize. Today it is taught by a number of ministers, who proclaim that it gives us hidden knowledge. The theory is an earmark of the teachings of southern California Pastor W. Eugene Scott, of Faith Center, in Glendale. Scott teaches the wonders of the pyramid's passageways, sometimes displaying elaborate drawings on his daily satellite television program, and ties it in with the stars and Stonehenge of England.

But perhaps a more serious concern about pyramidology is that those teaching or researching it draw upon sources proven to be cultic or occult for their inspiration. Take Whisenant, for example. In affirming that the pyramid has some type of prophetic significance (although from the wrong side of the fence)—accurately predicting dates of catastrophes such as the birth of communism and the creation of the Mormon church, which he claims were controlled by Satan—he drew upon a book by the late Spencer Lewis called *The Symbolic Prophecy of the Great Pyramid.*[11] But what Whisenant didn't mention was that Lewis was the first Imperator of the Ancient Mystical Order of Rosae Crucis (AMORC), the largest Rosicrucian order, the same group I saw in the pyramid that hot summer day.

Lewis taught pure heresy about Jesus Christ. He wrote that Christ was born of gentile parents "through whose veins flowed Aryan blood," that Jesus did not die on the cross, and that He didn't rise from the dead. Instead He retired to a monastery at Carmel, where he lived for many years and carried on secret sessions with His Apostles![12] The late Walter Martin, considered one of the twentieth century's leading cult experts, wrote that in Rosicrucianism, "everything Christian that it touches suffers violence at its hands."[13] Martin wrote:

> It is not only an eclectic theological system which mixes pagan mythology with Judaism and Christianity, with traces of Hinduism and Buddhism throughout, but it is a system of thinking which seeks to synthesize the basic truths of all religions and absorb them into a master system.[14]

"Revelations" of the Pyramids

Here are some of the last-days dates and times "revealed" by Bible-pyramid experts, measuring the various tunnels inside the Great Pyramid.

- A 1896 issue of the *Prophetic News and Israel Watchman* carried an article titled, "The Great Pyramid Pointing to About A.D. 1908 as the End of This Age and the Beginning of the Millennium."[15] Later another writer forecast 1928 to be the beginning of the Great Tribulation.[16] Lieutenant A. Kenney-Herbert of Great Britain said the pyramid indicated the Lord's return before 1944,[17] and David Davidson, the most prolific pyramidologist and perhaps the one most quoted by the Southwest Radio Church, picked 1953.[18]
- Others, too, set dates and backpedaled. One was Adam Rutherford, who established the Institute of Pyramidology in London. He also claimed the Great Pyramid revealed a 1953 date for the beginning of Christ's millennial king-

dom.[19] After that failed, he said it would "all end up in 1978–1979."[20]

- Also backpedaling were Webber and Hutchings. They wrote that 1992 is "probably" the "beginning of the Tribulation or the Abomination of Desolation to be committed by the Antichrist at the mid-way point of the Tribulation" and added "1996" might possibly be Christ's Second Coming.[21] But in an earlier version of the same book (issued eleven years earlier, under a different title), Webber and Hutchings stated that the pyramid seems to affirm other calculations, including the beginning of the tribulation to start in "1981–85" and the end of the tribulation (and by implication the Second Coming of Christ) in "1988–92."[22]
- Colin Deal wrote: "Scientists in this generation, using highly sophisticated technology, have discovered the pre-recorded prophetic data are registered in this monument [pyramid]. . . . The dates 1979 through 1989 are projected as important future dates. All signs are pointing to blast off."[23] But in his latest book, he changed his tune. Now the pyramid shows the establishment of "Christ's millennial Kingdom somewhere around 2000, give or take a few years."[24]

If we're counting the dozens of other date failures not covered here, the pyramidologists have more failed dates for Armageddon and the end of the age than even the Jehovah's Witnesses! Perhaps it's no coincidence that Jehovah's Witness founder Charles Taze Russell was deeply into pyramidology and an offshoot of that movement called the Layman's Home Missionary Movement (which still follows many of Russell's teachings) is deeply into pyramidology and produces detailed literature on the Great Pyramid being God's Bible in stone and its prophetic significance.[25]

Source of the Revelations

In 1859 a British writer named John Taylor put forth his theories that the architect of the Great Pyramid was not an

Egyptian. His book, *The Great Pyramid*, proposed that the pyramid's passageways and chambers were designed to indicate a prophetic and historic record that would echo biblical revelation. Just before him, Robert Menzies, of Scotland, proposed similar theories. Menzies said that the structure, rising 452 feet above the Egyptian desert sand, contained astronomical, chronological, and mathematical truth.[26]

Their theories really grabbed the public's fancy, especially after the renowned Scottish astronomer Piazzi Smyth (1819–1900) began looking into the matter. He became convinced of the theory and devoted much of the rest of his life to proving that the Great Pyramid of Giza had been divinely designed. Some thought his fascination with the pyramid was odd, considering he had an "almost feverish hatred for all the pagan temples and structures of ancient Egypt."[27]

A short time later Seiss and Bullinger got ahold of their ideas. Bullinger was so impressed with the Great Pyramid theories that he inserted various facts about it as commentary in *The Companion Bible*. He also worked aspects of the pyramid into various other writings, including *Number in Scripture*. Meanwhile Seiss, the translator of the hymn "Beautiful Saviour" into English, put forth his own theories about the Great Pyramid. Seiss wrote that the pyramid was built by Job, who could have really been Melchizedek, since he was called "the greatest of all the men of the east" (Job 1:3 KJV).[28]

David Davidson was another big name in pyramidology, but he came a bit later. Davidson was recognized as a leading authority on the prophetic interpretation of the pyramid,[29] and he remains so to this day, as the Southwest Radio Church and others continue to quote him liberally. One thing we haven't seen in print thus far from the prophecy teachers quoted in this chapter (other than Gene Scott) is that Davidson, Rutherford, and other pyramidologists identified themselves as Anglo-Israelites. They actively taught the idea that Great Britain and the English-speaking peoples—not the Jewish people who formed national Israel in 1948—are true Israel.[30] Davidson was also an early proponent of the idea, later taught by Deal, Southwest Church, and others, that the patriarch Enoch was probably the builder of the Great Pyramid.

But in this case most of the prophecy teachers have not mentioned—and there is evidence it may have been deliberately covered up—that the Enoch idea originated from an occult and possibly a demonic source—*The Egyptian Book of the Dead*.[31] The *Book of the Dead* is a series of instructions and magic spells for the pharaohs to use in the company of the gods in the afterlife.[32]

Speculation in Stone

There are many variations in the theories on how the Great Pyramid supposedly works in providing information about the future. But most pyramidologists believe the small shaft leading upward represents the Old Testament period of the *law* and the prophets. The point where the shaft opens up to a high ceiling represent's Christ's crucifixion, and the Grand Gallery represents the age of *grace*. Having direct access to the gallery is the Queen's Chamber, which represents *the church*. At the top of the gallery is a low doorway, which some believe represents the *great tribulation*, and the highest point, the King's Chamber, represents the *Second Coming of Christ* and the millennial kingdom. Of course, well beneath the pyramid is the pit, which represents *hell*. A large, descending passage leads to it, representing a *broad path to hell*. There is a small well shaft leading from the descending shaft to the Grand Gallery to represent a narrow *way of escape*.

The theory that the pyramid predicts dates for future events usually involves measuring the distance from the alleged crucifixion point to the King's Chamber. Many can't agree on whether an inch equals a year or some other combination. Many pyramidologists—almost always after the fact—claim they found 1914 or 1918—World War I, the Great Depression, and other events—via their tape measures.

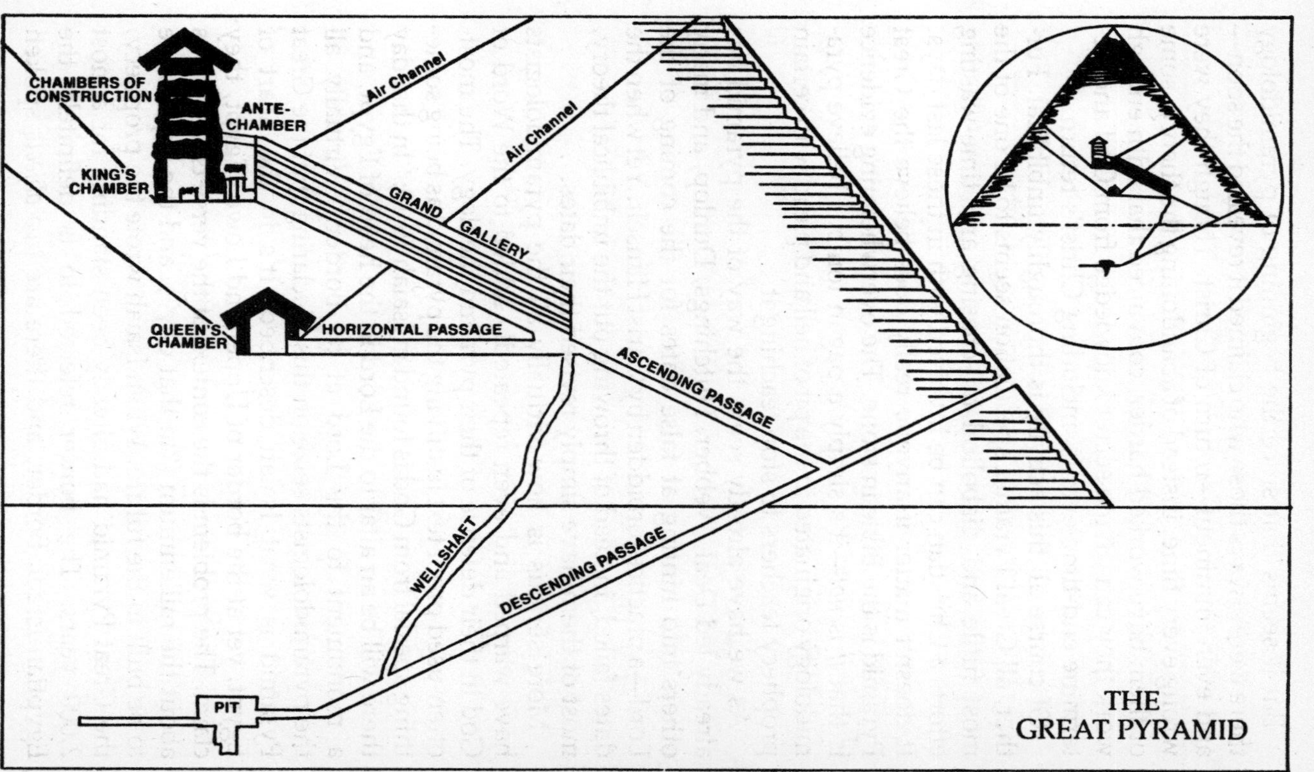
CHAMBERS OF
CONSTRUCTION
ANTE-
CHAMBER
KING'S
CHAMBER
Air Channel
Air Channel
GRAND GALLERY
QUEEN'S
CHAMBER
HORIZONTAL PASSAGE
ASCENDING PASSAGE
WELLSHAFT
DESCENDING PASSAGE
PIT
THE
GREAT PYRAMID

But it seems that since the beginning of pyramidology there were always those who claimed it revealed the soon—and even imminent—return of Christ. Though they were wrong every time, instead of abandoning the theory, some of them have worked harder, convinced that with enough work they can divine secret knowledge from God and determine end-time events, including Christ's return.

Of course all this activity is thoroughly unbiblical. Further, all Great Pyramid speculation seems to be one of the most futile and diabolical tail-chasing and time-wasting efforts a Christian can be involved with in these last days. It doesn't matter if anyone really does believe the Great Pyramid is the Bible in stone. The overwhelming evidence is that *it is not*—it's simply a pagan tomb. I believe pyramidology originated in the pit of hell and plead with certain prophecy teachers to stop teaching it.

As we have already seen, the way of the pyramid has already led Deal, Webber, Hutchings, Dunlop, and many others into hinting at false dates for the coming of the Lord—a practice forbidden by Christ Himself. Yet when the dates failed, instead of throwing out the unbiblical theory, most of them have simply revised their dates.

More serious is how virtually all the pyramidologists have warped and even repeatedly added to the Word of God in their defense of their pyramid theology. The most-often-used proof text justifying the pyramid as being something special from God is found in Isaiah 19:19: "In that day there will be an altar to the Lord in the heart of Egypt, and a monument to the Lord at its border." Virtually all the pyramidologists seize on this, declaring that the Great Pyramid is what Isaiah described. It's in the heart of Egypt, yet at the border of Upper and Lower Egypt, they claim. The problem is the context of the verse clearly talks about the millennium ("in that day"), and the objects are to be built in the future. When Isaiah wrote the prophecy, the Great Pyramid had already been standing for almost 2,000 years. The border referred to is definitely the Egyptian-Israeli border, and there are *two objects* spoken of—an altar and a monument, not one 452-foot tomb. (Since when is a pagan tomb an altar to a holy God?)

Other verses often cited are ones referring to Jesus being the capstone or those clearly referring to a capstone. But many of the capstone verses used (Psalm 118:22; Zechariah 4:7; Matthew 21:42; Acts 4:11; 1 Peter 2:7), clearly refer to the capstone of the Jewish temple in Jerusalem.

Speaking of the capstone, pyramidologists also make a big deal out of the Great Pyramid not having one. They claim it was rejected by the builders as a picture of Christ. But that's nonsense. Almost all Egyptologists believe the pyramid had a capstone at one time that was either taken as building material or possibly looted. Egyptologists point out that there were many Great Pyramid robberies, possibly ranging much further back than the birth of Christ. History already records that centuries ago the surface materials were excavated from the pyramid by the locals and used for building materials.

Pyramidologists' claim that there was never any body placed in the Great Pyramid is also open to question. They claim that the empty tomb pictures Christ's tomb being empty. Webber and Hutchings also suggested that it could have been empty because Enoch could have been Cheops, and after he was taken directly to heaven as the Scripture indicates in Genesis 5:24, the pyramid was sealed.[33] But it's a well-known fact that many bodies were stolen from the eighty or so pyramids in Egypt, so much so that the pharaohs stopped building them. Many of the later pharaohs built tombs—not pyramids—in the secret Valley of the Kings, hundreds of miles south, near the Nile, to thwart the robbers interested in the gold and treasures that accompanied their mummies.

The fact that there are many pyramids in Egypt brings us to another objection. Why was *only* the Great Pyramid considered divine? Although it is the largest one, many others, including the one just next to it, are almost as large. Bible pyramidologists have advanced the theory that the others were satanic copies of it, an example of the devil spreading confusion. (As if their pyramidology keeps with the simplicity of the Gospel!) But that's not a very good theory. There were many pyramids constructed *before* the great one.

A clear example of soothsayers' corrupting the Word of God is the contention by some that God referred to the Great Pyramid in the book of Job as the cornerstone of the world (Job 38:6, 7).[34]

Another main objection is stated well by Wilbur Smith:

> The builder of this Pyramid was no other than Cheops, as the monuments of Egypt testify, and there is not a shred of evidence anywhere in the Scriptures that this was the work of Enoch, Melchizedek, Job, or any other Biblical character. . . . Assigning the erection of the Great Pyramid to one of the patriarchs . . . represents one of the many fantastic ideas incorporated with the major piece of fancy, that the Pyramid has prophetic significance.[35]

In another point well taken, Smith said that building a "Bible in stone" goes against God's revealed will in the Scriptures and His plan that all the world would be reached through the Jews. The idea that "these vast tombs were built by idolatrous Gentiles who had no knowledge of the true God . . . is contrary to all we know of the methods God has used in revealing deeper truths to men," Smith wrote. Why did God withhold the "truth" of the pyramid "from his chosen prophets and from those who were ordained by Him to be the authors of the Holy Scriptures?"[36]

He also questioned the very theory that the structure "might contain chronological truth in the realm of prophecy." First, it's not in the Word of God. Second, out of three buildings erected in the Old Testament according to divine instruction, the tabernacle, the temple of Solomon's day, and the post-exilic temple, why don't any Bible scholars advance the idea that they have chronological prophecies?[37]

What about theories that the Great Pyramid really does reveal dates of important events? By working with figures enough, one can get the Great Pyramid—or any other structure—to reveal any date one wants it to reveal. One Christian scholar noted that the French scholar Bouisson debunked that theory partly by noting that if one were to subtract the number of those who partook of the Last Supper from 1,927 (the number of steps and landings in the Eiffel Tower) we come out with 1914, the date of the First World War.[38]

Part V
A Look Into the Future

As we consider the future—not in a highly speculative manner, but in a sane, biblically informed way—we need to consider our reactions to the teachings we've discussed. Do we really wish to allow ourselves to be led in all directions by the horror stories or fancies of a few? Or will we decide to close the prophetic portions of Scripture because we find them "too hard to understand" and don't want to get into controversial issues?

Neither of these options is right for the responsible Christian. God has given us prophecies to guide us in our Christian lives, especially in times like these. Though a few people may have abused that, we cannot avoid His commands merely out of a desire to be "safe."

If we know what the Scriptures—all the Scriptures—say about prophecy, and if we carefully discern what those who claim to have a word from God have based their teachings on, we can save ourselves much pain, and we can more effectually do the work God has left for us—until He comes!

19
Where It's All Leading To

South Carolina radio preacher Brother R. G. Stair was whipped into apocalyptic fever in early 1988. In his "Overcomer" radio broadcast, heard over fifty stations nationwide, he thundered that God has appointed him "God's end-time prophet to America," and that he had anointed the end-time "Elijah"—a young Russian man—several years earlier.

Furthermore, God had spoken directly to him, and the jig was up for America. Before "April" was over, the United States would face an economic collapse, followed by the forceable removal of President Ronald Reagan from office. Then a limited nuclear war would strike the United States before the end of the year, wiping out every major city.

A way to escape the horrors to come was to get out of the cities and flee to the countryside, Stair roared, sometimes altering his voice to sound as if God were speaking through him. Stair then announced that he was building "cities of refuge" (farms) throughout the rural south, from which the "remnant" could weather the great tribulation.

His radical claims struck a chord. People from all over the United States began selling their homes and started sending money to Stair's Faith Cathedral Fellowship, located near Walterboro, South Carolina. As contributions came in Stair was able to extend his daily message of fear to almost 100 radio stations nationwide.

In Philadelphia three local churches eagerly tuned in to the message, and parishioners started selling their possessions. Before May was out, about ten church members joined Stair at his commune, turning all their money over to him in exchange for living quarters in his commune. Obviously the economy didn't collapse, Reagan finished his term, and doomsday never came. Despite the failures, many of Stair's new converts stayed with him, accepting his explanation that God had changed His mind.

But one couple that exited, months after joining, left deeply wounded. The wife had joined Stair's commune while she was well along in her pregnancy, and Stair had discouraged the use of medicine and modern doctors. As a result the couple's ten-pound, twelve-ounce baby boy was born dead in Stair's commune on July 6 at the hands of unlicensed midwives—sect members. The next day Colleton County Coroner Bob Bryan investigated the death and ruled the baby died of "anoxia," or an absence of oxygen caused by a prolonged delivery. Though no criminal charges were filed, he ruled the death could have been prevented.

My wife and I covered the unfolding story of this cult for the *Delaware County Daily Times*, in Upper Darby, Pennsylvania; we wrote more than thirty stories on Stair and the local doomsday cults seeking to join him.[1] Two things became very clear as we researched the stories: It was Stair's message of fear that seemed to draw his followers, and he reinforced that fear through his monthly newsletters. Among the fantastic stories it contained were:

Descriptions of the "New Age conspiracy."
Accounts of the coming Antichrist.
Tales of the "Beast computer" in Brussels.
References to fiber-optic wires, connected to your television set, that could allow the Antichrist to control your life, watch

> you twenty-four hours a day, and kill you in your own home.[2]

A lot of that may sound familiar—much of Stair's material came from prophecy teachers we've talked about. In the March, 1988, issue, Stair even used one of Southwest Radio Church's photographs and reprinted part of their article to scare people into believing the three-story "Beast computer" is already here.

However, becoming disillusioned with biblical prophecy because of people like Brother Stair does not solve our problem with prophecy. After all, about 30 percent of God's Word is prophecy. Do we really want to ignore one-third of the Bible?

Throwing Prophecy Out with the Bath Water?

Yes, there have been many false and ill-advised interpretations of biblical prophecy, and we have to be careful what we believe. After all, Christianity has never said that you should accept everything you hear—that's in no way a biblical principle. But neither should you give up in despair when you see the results of false prophecies. After all, doesn't God promise to bring confusion to those who so misapply His Word?

Jesus Is *Coming!*

Despite all the date setting, prediction, and speculation, nothing can change the fact that Jesus *will* come. He promises it in His Word; and just as He came the first time, fulfilling a host of prophecies, He will come again, fulfilling many more.

After the Ascension, the angels told the Apostles, ". . . This same Jesus, who has been taken from you into heaven, will come back in the same way you have seen him go into heaven" (Acts 1:11). We cannot ignore or overspiritualize His Second Coming. Instead we need to look for Him, as Jesus Himself told His disciples: " 'Keep watch, because you do not know on what day your Lord will come. . . . So you also must be ready, because the Son of Man will come at an hour when you do not expect him' " (Matthew 24:42, 44).

A Wise Christian Response to Date Setters

Picture yourself living in the year 2010, and imagine that Christ has not yet returned. Will you throw out your faith because you believed He would come back before the year 2000? If prophecy teachers continue to proclaim that the coming of the Lord will occur around the year 2000, there may be a lot more laughter and scoffing if it doesn't happen. Could this lead to more defections from the faith?

There is time to head off some of the scoffing and the alienation that results from a failed prophecy. Responsible prophecy teachers need to make a pact to carefully investigate all prophecy statements, so the truths of the Lord's Second Coming will not suffer ill repute, and then take date setters to task. The ministries spreading dangerous, false rumors about the end times must be stopped. Perhaps we need to heed this biblical injunction: "They must be silenced, because they are ruining whole households by teaching things they ought not to teach—and that for the sake of dishonest gain" (Titus 1:11).

I think all prophecy teachers and ministers who teach prophecy should sign the "Manifesto on Date Setting," drafted in 1988 by Springfield, Missouri, prophecy teacher David A. Lewis. It states:

> Whereas the Scripture clearly says that no man can know the day or hour of the Lord's coming, thus indicating that date setting serves no good purpose,
>
> And whereas date setting has historically always proven to be false prophecy which is damaging to the cause of Christ
>
> And whereas we are living in the last days and

nothing must be allowed to detract from the nobility and power of the message of end-time Bible prophecy

> Therefore we, the undersigned hereby demand that all date setting and date suggesting cease immediately. Let abstinence from this type of speculation prevail until the Lord comes.
>
> We absolutely must stop this type of activity or there will be few who will take the message of prophecy seriously.
>
> If Jesus should tarry until the year 2000 we envision that by 2001 the message of Bible prophecy will be scorned, attacked and possibly outlawed by legal means—thus giving the New Age Movement a clear field for the introduction of their occult humanist messiah.[3]

20
"Blessed Is the One Who Reads"

In November, 1886, Christian theologians from around the world gathered together in Chicago for the Prophetic Studies of the International Prophetic Conference, to exchange ideas about the long-neglected subject of eschatology. World-renowned Bible teacher D. L. Moody sent in his contribution, being unable to attend personally. The speeches were gathered in a one-volume book. The preface reads:

> The conference gave no opportunity for modern prophets to ventilate their calculations or speculations. It was rather an occasion for students of prophecy to present the weighty matters found in the written word concerning "last times" and "last things." The brethren who were appointed to bring to the conference the results of prayerful and careful Bible study are neither idle star-gazers, erratic time-setters, nor theological adventurers.[1]

These men understood the importance of correctly handling the word of truth with reverence, " '. . . for the testimony of Jesus is the spirit of prophecy' " (Revelation 19:10). Without prophecy, we would have no Bible. If the devil could discredit Bible prophecy, he could eliminate Christianity.

Because of the carelessness of the soothsayers today, many Christian leaders have thrown the baby out with the bath water and have discouraged their flocks from reading the book of Revelation and other prophetic books of the Bible.

Prophecy teacher David Lewis laments, "The tragedy is that the message [of prophecy] has been attacked by its enemies, eroded by its friends and ignored by everybody else."[2]

Yet the book of Revelation comes with a blessing for those who read it: "Blessed is the one who reads the words of this prophecy, and blessed are those who hear it and take to heart what is written in it, because the time is near" (Revelation 1:3).

The remarkable accuracy of the Bible in foretelling the future is one of the proofs that the Bible is God's inspired Word. Since the Old Testament prophecies concerning Christ's first coming were fulfilled to the letter, we can have confidence that the prophecies related to His return and the inauguration of the 1,000-year millennial age will take place.

When my wife was a nonbeliever, it never occurred to her to read the Bible. She thought it was an outdated book with no relevance for today, just full of old-fashioned "thou shalt nots." When she heard that the Bible taught that Jesus was going to return to planet earth in the not-so-distant future, she realized that Christianity wasn't just a religion of the past.

The discovery that God had a preordained plan for the consummation of the ages caused her to reconsider the claims of the Bible. Somehow knowing that the many authors of the Bible accurately foretold events that had taken place in her day proved its divine origin. After brushing the cobwebs off her Bible, she came face-to-face with the person of Jesus Christ, who alone could bring her safely into His kingdom.

So the prophetic message brought her hope for the future in spite of the fearful events taking place all around her. Having put her trust in the God who controls the future, she no longer had to be afraid of bringing children into a world she thought was on the brink of destruction. She could latch on to the promise given to the church in Philadelphia, "Since you have kept my command to endure patiently, I will also keep you from the hour of trial that is going to come upon the whole world to test those who live on the earth" (Revelation 3:10).

So Bible prophecy is a faith builder, and living during a time that is witnessing the "beginning of sorrows" need not frighten the child of God. The signs of the times serve as a reminder to continue to contend for the faith and enter boldly into every open door for evangelism, while there is still time. We are instructed by the Word of God to keep alert and watch for the return of the Bridegroom. The anticipation itself transforms and purifies our lives: ". . . We know that when he appears, we shall be like him, for we shall see him as he is. Everyone who has this hope in him purifies himself . . ." (1 John 3:2, 3).

David Lewis summarized what our attitude toward the Second Coming of Jesus Christ should be: "It is better to live as if Jesus were coming today and yet prepare for the future as if He were not coming for a long time. Then you are ready for time and eternity."[3]

Many scoffers of Bible prophecy point out the fact that throughout church history groups have come and gone who have claimed that Jesus was to return in their day. That may well be true; however if they lived with the daily expectancy of their Lord's arrival, then their hope was not in vain and their lives reflected the good fruit of their faith.

But today *is* different from the past 2,000 years for one very good reason: the return of the Jews to the land of Israel. Before this historic event took place, the prophecies of the end times *could not* occur. So in a sense all ancient speculations were invalid—and careless. Biblical literalists predicted the return of the Jews long before it became a reality in 1948.

James J. Brookes, in his 1878 book, *Maranatha or the Lord Cometh,* cited Jeremiah's prophecy of the restoration of the Jews to their land and pointed out:

> Their dispersion is conditional, made to depend upon their obedience, but, blessed be God, their restoration is unconditional, made to depend upon His sovereign grace and unchangeable purpose. . . . Turning . . . to Jeremiah, we find numerous predictions of utter desolation coming upon Judah and Jerusalem and all Israel for the sins of the people, foretelling the seventy years of captivity in Babylon, their partial restoration, their continued iniquity, their banishment into all countries, and their final return in connection with the glorious advent and reign of their Messiah.[4]

This literal fulfillment of Bible prophecy, coupled with the ever-increasing signs of the times, tells us we should lift up our heads, for our redemption is drawing near (Luke 21:28).

There's no need to reach for the *National Enquirer* or to turn on the "Morton Downey Jr. Show" to find the signs of the times. They are all around us. Jesus gave a description of the condition of the world just prior to His return, in Matthew 24:37: " 'As it was in the days of Noah, so it will be at the coming of the Son of Man.' " The days of Noah are described in Genesis 6:5: "The Lord saw how great man's wickedness on the earth had become, and that every inclination of the thoughts of his heart was only evil all the time."

In Matthew 24 Jesus predicts an increase of wickedness (v. 12), after saying, " 'Many false prophets will appear and deceive many people' " (v. 11). He warns of false Christs that will perform great signs and miracles in order to deceive (v. 24). He describes wars and rumors of wars, nation rising against nation, as well as famines and earthquakes all coming upon the earth like birth pangs upon a woman in labor.

The future tribulation is described in verses 21 and 22:

> For then there will be great distress, unequaled from the beginning of the world until now—and never to be equaled again. If those days had not been cut short, no one would survive, but for the sake of the elect those days will be shortened.

The Lord promises to intervene before mankind destroys himself and the planet. So when we hear about the horrors of the greenhouse effect, the hole in the ozone layer, the air, land, and water pollution, we can rest, knowing that God will eventually deliver this planet from the destroyers.

To many this may sound negative. But one only has to watch the daily newscast to get even more alarmed at the increase in wickedness. The rise in brutal crime is startling. The popularity of slasher-type violent movies appeals to the same brutality in man that was evident in the Roman coliseum, when the Christians were thrown to lions amidst the cheers of the spectators. In our society it's quite legal for doctors to kill babies in their mother's wombs, even though they are prosecuted for murder when the aborted babies are delivered alive and allowed to die. Evidence of the increase of evil is only too obvious.

Dave Hunt defends true Bible prophecy:

> The Great Tribulation and Armageddon leading up to Christ's justified and necessary intervention on planet earth to stop the destruction and set up His kingdom are also part of God's outworking of His will in human history. These events are clearly prophesied in Scripture, and to present them as a warning to the

> world is not "gloom and doom" but simply faithfulness to the truth.[5]

The time is coming when all the things the prophets spoke of will come to pass with 100 percent accuracy. There is coming seven years of the greatest tribulation man has ever seen. Man's arch-enemy the devil will take possession of a man known as the Antichrist, and his false prophet will cause the whole world to come under a one-world economic system, using a mark on the hand or forehead in order to buy or sell.

We may be closer to that time than we think. The world is headed toward Armageddon, and the signs of the times indicate that we are speedily rushing toward the final chapter of history, although we cannot know the exact day or hour. The person destined to be the false messiah, the Antichrist, *could* be alive today. The European Economic Community could well be the power base from which the Antichrist will arise. The Soviet Union could even be "Gog," described in Ezekiel 38, and someday—perhaps sooner than we think—her vast army could invade Israel and be destroyed. Or it might be another, as yet unidentified, nation.

No doubt these events *will* occur to some generation at some time and will come upon the world like a thief in the night. But we are told we will know when it's even at the door (but we will not know the day or the hour or even the times and the seasons), and we are told to watch and pray and occupy until He returns. We as Christians have this assurance: "But you, brothers, are not in darkness so that this day should surprise you like a thief. You are all sons of the light and sons of the day . . . (1 Thessalonians 5:4, 5).

Just because some have improperly used Bible prophecy for soothsaying and sensationalism doesn't mean we should abandon the study of eschatology. Rather we need to rescue it and use it as an encouragement as we see the signs increase. The Word of God will not fail; every jot and tittle will be fulfilled, or else our Bible has errors and is worthless. We can trust God when He declares: " 'I make known the end from the beginning, from ancient times, what is still to come. I say: My purpose will stand, and I will do all that I please' " (Isaiah 46:10).

The Good News

Although I have focused on prophecy error, the good news is that many good prophecy teachers around today don't play fast and loose with the truth. Although I don't think Hal Lindsey should have implied a forty-year generation between the creation of Israel and the rapture, in his classic book, *The Late Great Planet Earth*, this prophecy book and others he has written still have much value in them. (It is also true that Lindsey agrees with this. He has publicly stated that he was premature in setting a time limit on a generation.) It is amazing that this twenty-year-old book remains as relevant today as it was when it was written.

In a recent issue of *Moody Monthly*, Garry Friesen reevaluated *Late Great* upon Israel's forty-year anniversary and noted, "Rereading *Late Great*, however, has reminded me of its power. It communicated a complex subject so well that both believers and unbelievers kept turning the pages and opening their Bibles."[6]

Only eternity will reveal how many people came to know Jesus Christ as a result of reading that book. According to the *Moody* article, more than 25 million copies have been printed in thirty languages, and the book is in its one hundredth printing.

Speaking of the last generation, according to God's Word, He does not want any to perish, and He is long-suffering (2 Peter 3:9). His delay is grace to the unbelievers. Even as the last days are compared to the days of Noah, it is interesting to note that the flood occurred after the death of Methuselah, the longest-living person in history. God in His mercy allowed Methuselah to live just under 1,000 years, and then the flood came.

God has the divine option to do the same for our generation. When Peter asked Jesus what He would do with John the Beloved, Jesus responded, " 'If I want him to remain alive until I return, what is that to you? . . .' " (John 21:22). God is quite able to do that today if He indeed meant the fig tree to represent the restoration of the Jews to the land of Israel. So in Matthew 24:34, when Jesus said ". . . this generation will certainly not pass away until all these things have happened," He wasn't bound by the normal life expectancy of man.

With that much said, I can recommend most works of other prophecy teachers like John Walvoord, David Lewis, David Breese, Chuck Smith, and others.

I hope the ministries examined in this book will not allow a perceived attack to prevent them from reevaluating their unscriptural practices. More than anything I wish to see them use their considerable talents in a balanced way that honors God and His Word. In Matthew 24:44 Christ said He'll come ". . . at an hour when you do not expect him." As long as soothsayers predict dates, He'll not likely return on those dates. The Scriptures teach that He will not allow the word of a soothsayer to come to pass regarding His plans:

> ". . . I am the Lord who has made all things, who alone stretched out the heavens, who spread out the earth by myself, who foils the signs of false prophets and makes fools of diviners, who overthrows the learning of the wise and turns it into nonsense, who carries out the words of his servants and fulfills the predictions of his messengers, who says of Jerusalem, 'It shall be inhabited,' of the towns of Judah, 'They shall be built,' and of their ruins, 'I will restore them.' "
>
> Isaiah 44:24–26

Since the heart of God desires that none should perish, but that all should come to repentance, we should have this same attitude—hoping that the door of grace will remain open long enough for our loved ones to be saved. We certainly don't wish the great tribulation to come upon those we love.

Many soothsayers, instead of admitting their error in setting dates for the rapture, claim that God simply changed His mind as He did with Jonah at Nineveh. Of course, after the great fish spit Jonah onto the ground, and he prophesied destruction to Nineveh, the people *repented* in sackcloth and ashes and begged for God's forgiveness. The Lord relented. Jeremiah understood God's justice and wrote:

> "If at any time I announce that a nation or kingdom is to be uprooted, torn down and destroyed, and if that nation I warned repents of its evil, then I will relent and not inflict on it the disaster I had planned. And if at another time I announce that a nation or kingdom is to be built up and planted, and if it does evil in my sight and does not obey me, then I will reconsider the good I had intended to do for it."
>
> Jeremiah 18:7–10

The Scriptures do not give license to date setters or visionaries with divine messages to fall back on Jonah to explain away their rash calculations—not unless there is repentance.

Soothsayers also often misuse Amos 3:7 to justify their date setting: "Surely the Sovereign Lord does nothing without revealing his plan to his servants the prophets." Those using this passage fail to see that God has already revealed the events of the end to His servant, the Apostle John on the Island of Patmos, and before him, the other Apostles. After showing John what would happen in the last days, the angel gave a solemn warning:

> I warn everyone who hears the words of the prophecy of this book: If anyone adds anything to them, God will add to him the plagues described in this book. And

> if anyone takes words away from this book of prophecy, God will take away from him his share in the tree of life and in the holy city, which are described in this book.
>
> Revelation 22:18, 19

With such a dire warning, it would be advisable for today's soothsayers and prophets to take heed before carelessly proclaiming, "thus saith the Lord," when referring to extrabiblical revelation concerning the coming of the Lord and His judgments.

There would not be soothsayers and unbiblical sensationalists today if a ready audience did not demand their teachings. Those who seek after unbiblical revelation and are not satisfied with studying God's Word are just as responsible for the Bible being discredited. This prophecy has indeed been fulfilled in our day:

> For the time will come when men will not put up with sound doctrine. Instead, to suit their own desires, they will gather around them a great number of teachers to say what their itching ears want to hear. They will turn their ears away from the truth and turn aside to myths.
>
> 2 Timothy 4:3, 4

So when will the Lord return? At the end of the age " '. . . you will see the Son of Man sitting on the right hand of the Mighty One and coming on the clouds of heaven' " (Matthew 26:64).

Questions or comments concerning the subject matter of this book should be addressed to:

William and Jacqueline Alnor
P.O. Box 11322
Philadelphia, PA 19137

We are also interested in receiving news tips on Bible prophecy, date setting, and other controversial issues affecting the church.

Please enclose a self-addressed, stamped envelope.

Notes

Introduction

1. "Rapture Seer Hedges on Latest Guess," *Christianity Today* (October 12, 1988), 43.
2. Steven Lawson, "Edgar Whisenant: His New Predictions," *Charisma & Christian Life* (February, 1989), 58.
3. Charles Taylor, *Those Who Remain* (Huntington Beach, Calif.: Today in Bible Prophecy, 1980), 10.

Chapter 1

1. David Webber, *Countdown for Antichrist* (Oklahoma City, Okla.: Southwest Radio Church, 1976), 15.
2. David Webber and N. W. Hutchings, *Countdown for Antichrist*, rev. ed. (Oklahoma City: Southwest Radio Church, 1984), 121.
3. *Gospel Truth* (June, 1987), 3.
4. Noah Hutchings, "The Vatican Connection," *Gospel Truth* (April, 1984), 4.
5. Constance E. Cumbey, *A Planned Deception: The Staging of a New Age "Messiah"* (East Detroit, Mich.: Pointe Publishers, 1985), 9.
6. "Rebuilding the Wall" conference tapes (Phoenix, Ariz.: First Century Ministries, March 19–21, 1987).
7. Constance E. Cumbey, "Special Report on Pat Robertson," *New Age Monitor* (August–December, 1987), 13, 14.
8. Charles Taylor, *Those Who Remain* (Huntington Beach, Calif.: Today in Bible Prophecy, 1980), 77.
9. Charles Taylor, *When Jesus Comes* (Huntington Beach, Calif.: Today in Bible Prophecy, 1985), 14.
10. Mary S. Relfe, *When Your Money Fails . . . the "666 System" Is Here* (Montgomery, Ala.: Ministries, 1981), cover.
11. Mary S. Relfe, *The New Money System* (Montgomery, Ala.: Ministries, 1982), 132.
12. Ibid.

13. R. Henry Hall, *AD 1991—The Genesis of Holocaust* (Las Vegas, Nev.: Spirit of Prophecy Evangelical Ministries, 1985), 53.
14. William M. Alnor, "Apocalypse Soon?" Today Magazine, *Philadelphia Inquirer* (April 12, 1981), 34.
15. Webber, *Countdown*, 23.
16. Relfe, *Money Fails*, cover.

Chapter 2

1. Edgar C. Whisenant, *On Borrowed Time* (Nashville, Tenn.: World Bible Society, 1988), foreword.
2. J. R. Church, *Hidden Prophecies in the Psalms* (Oklahoma City: Prophecy Publications, 1986), 246, 247.
3. Hart Armstrong, "Till There Is No Remedy," tract 43222 (Wichita, Ks.: Christian Communications, 1988), 12.
4. *Bible Prophecy News* 16, no. 4 (October, November, December, 1987), 12.
5. *Bible Prophecy News* 17, no. 1 (January, February, March, 1988), 11.
6. "Rapture Seer Hedges on Latest Guess," *Christianity Today* (October 21, 1988), 43.
7. Steven Lawson, "Edgar Whisenant: His New Predictions," *Charisma & Christian Life* (February, 1989), 60.
8. *World* (April 15, 1989), 11.
9. Dean C. Halverson, "88 Reasons What Went Wrong," *Christian Research Journal* (Fall, 1988), 15, 16.
10. Lawson, "Edgar Whisenant," 59.
11. Halverson, "88 Reasons," 16.
12. Lawson, "Edgar Whisenant," 60.

Chapter 3

1. Mary Stewart Relfe, *Economic Advisor* (February 28, 1983).
2. Ibid.
3. Whisenant, *On Borrowed Time* (Nashville, Tenn.: World Bible Society, 1988), 48.
4. Ibid. However, in Whisenant's new book, *The Final Shout. Rapture Report 1989* (Nashville, Tenn.: World Bible Society, 1989), 24, he has further revised his tribulation chart. For example, the Antichrist's death is listed at April 9, 1993, and World War III is scheduled to begin September 22, 1989.
5. Reginald E. Dunlop, *The Coming Russian Invasion of America—Why? When? Where?* (Ontario, Calif.: Reginald Dunlop, 1977), 318.

6. Ibid., 327.
7. Ibid., 318.
8. Ibid., 297.
9. Ibid., 304.
10. David Webber and Noah Hutchings, *Prophecy in Stone* (Fort Worth, Tex.: Harvest Press, 1974), 65.
11. David Webber and Noah Hutchings, *New Light on the Great Pyramid* (Oklahoma City: Southwest Radio Church, 1985), 65.
12. Interview with David Webber and Noah Hutchings on April 19, 1989.
13. David Webber and Noah Hutchings, *Is This the Last Century?* (Nashville, Tenn.: Thomas Nelson, 1979), 49.
14. David Webber and Noah Hutchings, *Gospel Truth* (June, 1987), 1.
15. Colin Deal, *Christ Returns by 1988: 101 Reasons Why* (Rutherford College, N.C.: Colin Deal, 1979), 158.
16. Ibid., 169.
17. Colin H. Deal, *The Day and Hour Jesus Will Return* (Rutherford College, N.C.: Colin Deal, 1981), 113.
18. Ibid., 117.
19. *Pat Robertson's Perspective* (February/March, 1980), 5.
20. Lester Sumrall, *I Predict 2000 A.D.* (South Bend, Ind.: LeSEA Publishing Co., 1987), 74.
21. Mary Stewart Relfe, *Economic Advisor* (February 28, 1983).
22. Chuck Smith, *Future Survival* (Costa Mesa, Calif.: Calvary Chapel, 1978), 20.
23. Interview with Chuck Smith on March 30, 1989.

Chapter 4

1. James J. Brookes, *Maranatha or the Lord Cometh* (St. Louis: Edward Bredell, 1878), 94.
2. Ibid., 25, 26.
3. Arthur E. Bloomfield, *Before the Last Battle Armageddon* (Minneapolis, Minn.: Bethany House Publishers, 1971), 16.
4. Brookes, *Maranatha*, 26, 27.
5. Hal Lindsey, *The Late Great Planet Earth*, 36th ed. (New York: Bantam, 1981), 10, 11.
6. Ibid., 12, 13.
7. Ibid., 13, 15.
8. Ibid., 160.
9. Brookes, *Maranatha*, 398.
10. Ibid., 396.

11. Ibid., 81.
12. Lindsey, *Late Great*, 160.

Chapter 5

1. Norman Cohn, *The Pursuit of the Millennium*, 2nd ed. (New York: Harper Torchbooks, 1961), 21.
2. Ibid., 9.
3. Ibid.
4. Ibid., 14.
5. Ibid., 9.
6. James J. Brookes, *Maranatha or the Lord Cometh* (Saint Louis: Edward Bredell, 1878), 364.
7. Cohn, *Pursuit*, 75.
8. Ibid., 106.
9. Ibid., 224.
10. William M. Alnor, "Apocalypse Soon?" Today Magazine, *The Philadelphia Inquirer* (April 12, 1981), 16.
11. Cohn, *Pursuit*, 275.
12. Richard Heath, *Anabaptism: From Its Rise at Zwickau to Its Fall at Munster, 1521–1536* (London: Alexander and Shepherd, 1895), 119.
13. Robert L. Christian, "Communities of Millennium: A Term Paper" (Empire State College, April, 1980), 13.
14. Leon Festinger, Henry W. Reicken, and Stanley Schachter, *When Prophecy Fails* (Minneapolis: University of Minnesota Press, 1956), 13.
15. Alnor, "Apocalypse," 18.
16. C. E. Sears, *Days of Delusion—a Strange Bit of History* (New York: Houghton Mifflin, 1924), 144.

Chapter 6

1. Doug Clark, *When Planets Align . . . (SYZTGY) EARTHQUAKE 1982!!* (Garden Grove, Calif.: Lyfe Production Publication, 1976), 9.
2. Ibid., 79.
3. Ibid., 28.
4. Ibid., 28.
5. Ibid., 39. *Emphasis added.*
6. John R. Gribbin and Stephen Plagemann, *The Jupiter Effect* (New York: Walker Publishing Co., 1974), 116.
7. Hal Lindsey, *Countdown to Armageddon*, long-playing record, 1980.
8. Pat Robertson, *Pat Robertson's Perspective* (February/March, 1980), 3.

9. Emil Gaverluk, *Gospel Truth* (September, 1979).
10. David Webber and Noah Hutchings, *Is This the Last Century?* (Nashville, Tenn.: Thomas Nelson, 1979), 123.
11. David F. Webber and Noah Hutchings, *Apocalyptic Signs in the Heavens* (Oklahoma City: Southwest Radio Church, 1979), 64.
12. Interview with Noah Hutchings on April 19, 1989.
13. James McKeever, *Christians Will Go Through the Tribulation*, 6th ed. (Medford, Ore.: Omega Publications, 1980), 163.
14. *End Times News Digest* (August, 1981), 12.
15. Telephone interview with Doug Clark on April 11, 1989.
16. David Ritchie, *Comets—The Swords of Heaven* (New York: Plume, 1985), 42.
17. Mary Stewart Relfe, Relfe's newsletter (April 30, 1981), 8.
18. Colin Deal, *Christ Returns by 1988: 101 Reasons Why* (Rutherford College, N.C.: Colin Deal, 1979), 134, 135.
19. Chuck Smith, *Future Survival* (Costa Mesa, Calif.: Calvary Chapel, 1978), 20.
20. *End Times News Digest* (March, 1983), 10.
21. Constance E. Cumbey, *A Planned Deception: The Staging of a New Age "Messiah"* (East Detroit, Mich.: Pointe Publishers, 1985), 9.
22. Interview with Frank Maloney, Villanova University, March 28, 1989.
23. Webber, *Gospel Truth* (January, 1986), 3.
24. Webber and Hutchings, *Apocalyptic Signs*, 21–22.

Chapter 7

1. Colin Deal, *Christ Returns by 1988: 101 Reasons Why* (Rutherford College: Colin Deal, 1979), 83.
2. Ibid., 81.
3. Ibid., 85, 86.
4. *Gospel Truth* 17, no. 12 (November, 1977), 5, 6.
5. Emil Gaverluk and Patrick Fisher, *Fiber Optics: The Eye of Antichrist* (Oklahoma City: Southwest Radio Church, 1979), 11.
6. *Awakeners Newsletter*, 1.
7. James McKeever, *End Times News Digest* (September, 1981), 1.
8. Charles Taylor, "666" tract.
9. Interview with Charles Taylor on April 24, 1989.
10. Report on Doug Clark's February 5, 1984, seminar, filed with the Christian Research Institute, San Juan Capistrano, Calif.
11. Interview with James McKeever on April 20, 1989.

Chapter 8

1. Mary S. Relfe, *When Your Money Fails . . . the "666 System" Is Here* (Montgomery, Ala.: Ministries, 1981), 143–145.
2. Mary Stewart Relfe, *The New Money System* (Montgomery, Ala.: Ministries, 1982), copyright page.
3. Relfe, *Money Fails*, 134.
4. Ibid., 17.
5. Ibid., 19.
6. Ibid., 15.
7. Ibid., 30.
8. Ibid., 27.
9. Ibid., 26.
10. Ibid., 16.
11. James McKeever, *End Time News Digest* (September, 1981), 1.

Chapter 9

1. Fawn Vrazo, "Killer Bees Closing in on S. Texas," *Philadelphia Inquirer* (April 22, 1987), 5A.
2. Ibid.
3. Salem Kirban, *Countdown to Rapture* (Huntingdon Valley, Penn.: Salem Kirban, 1977), 27.
4. Harold A. Sevener, "Are Vultures Gathering in Israel for the Battle of Armageddon?" *Chosen People* (October, 1980), 12.
5. David Webber and Noah Hutchings, *Is This the Last Century?* (Nashville, Tenn.: Thomas Nelson, 1979), 16, 17. The authors report that they "have not been able . . . to document this occurrence in Israel."
6. Hart Armstrong, "The Mark of the Beast; Is It on Earth Now?" tract 43012.
7. Interview with James McKeever on April 20, 1989.
8. Mary S. Relfe, *When Your Money Fails . . . the "666 System" Is Here* (Montgomery, Ala.: Ministries, 1981), 69.
9. Ibid., 30.
10. Interview with Charles Taylor on April 24, 1989.
11. Constance Cumbey, *The Hidden Dangers of the Rainbow* (Shreveport, La.: Huntington House, 1983), 116.
12. Charles R. Taylor, *Beware America—A Message to the President* (Huntington Beach, Calif.: Today in Bible Prophecy, 1983), 25, 26.
13. David Webber and Noah Hutchings, *Apocalyptic Signs in the Heavens* (Oklahoma City: Southwest Radio Church, 1979), 61.
14. David Webber, *Gospel Truth* (January, 1986), 4.

15. *Gospel Truth* (June, 1987), 2.
16. *Bible Prophecy News* 16 (October, November, December, 1987), 2.
17. Edgar C. Whisenant, *88 Reasons Why the Rapture Could Be in 1988* (Nashville, Tenn.: World Bible Society, 1988), 68, 69.
18. "Praise the Lord" program, April 26, 1989, on Trinity Broadcasting Network.
19. Emil Gaverluk and Patrick Fisher, *Fiber Optics: The Eye of the Antichrist* (Oklahoma City: Southwest Radio Church, 1979), introduction.
20. Ibid., 22.
21. Relfe, *Money Fails,* 119–126.
22. Salem Kirban, *I Predict* (Iowa Falls, Iowa: Riverside Book and Bible House, 1970), 114–136.
23. Statement issued by Salem Kirban, dated March 28, 1989, in response to my questions about his work.

Chapter 10

1. Carl O. Dunbar, *Historical Geology* (New York: John Wiley and Sons, 1949), 21.
2. Edgar C. Whisenant, *88 Reasons Why the Rapture Could Be in 1988* (Nashville, Tenn.: World Bible Society, 1988), 22.
3. Ralph Woodrow, *His Truth Is Marching On: Advanced Studies on Prophecy in the Light of History* (Riverside, Calif.: Ralph Woodrow Evangelistic Association, 1977), 22.
4. Ibid.
5. R. Henry Hall, *AD 1991—The Genesis of Holocaust* (Las Vegas, Nev.: Spirit of Prophecy Evangelical Ministries, 1985), 44, 45.
6. Reginald E. Dunlop, *The Coming Russian Invasion of America—Why? When? Where?* (Ontario, Calif.: Reginald Dunlop, 1977), 301–304.
7. Hart Armstrong, "Just Suppose," tract 42903 (Wichita, Ks.: Christian Communications, 1988), 5–7.
8. *End Times News Digest* (February, 1983), 5.
9. Colin Deal, *Christ Returns by 1988: 101 Reasons Why,* 5th ed. (Rutherford College, N.C.: Colin Deal, 1979), 165, 166.
10. J. R. Church, *Hidden Prophecies in the Psalms* (Oklahoma City: Prophecy Publications, 1986), 274.
11. Ibid., 266.
12. *Gospel Truth* (June, 1987), 3.
13. David Webber, *Countdown for Antichrist* (Oklahoma City, Okla.: Southwest Radio Church, 1976), 22.
14. Mary S. Relfe, *When Your Money Fails . . . the "666 System" Is Here* (Montgomery, Ala.: Ministries, 1981), 133.

15. Interview with Ken Ham on January 11, 1989.
16. Steve Stecklow, "Marvels Underground," *Philadelphia Inquirer* (December 18, 1988), 1-R.
17. Paul A. Zimmerman, *Rock Strata and the Biblical Record* (St. Louis: Concordia Publishing House, 1970), 57, 58.
18. Ibid., 58–60.
19. Ibid., 60, 61.
20. Ibid., 62.
21. Ibid.
22. Ibid.
23. Ibid., 63.
24. Taped interview with Grant R. Jeffrey aired on the Southwest Radio Church, April 20, 1989.

Chapter 11

1. David Webber, *Satan's Kingdom and the Second Coming* (Oklahoma City: Southwest Radio Church, undated [circa 1973]), 38.
2. David Webber, *A Satanic Trilogy: Pyramid Power* (Oklahoma City: Southwest Radio Church, 1975), 14–17.
3. "Entire State of Rhode Island Changes by Mind Power Test," *Bible in the News* (September, 1979), 9.
4. Interview with Noah Hutchings on April 19, 1989.
5. Emil Gaverluk, *The Rapture in the Old Testament* (Oklahoma City: Southwest Radio Church, 1986), 25, 26.
6. David Webber and Noah Hutchings, *Apocalyptic Signs in the Heavens* (Oklahoma City: Southwest Radio Church, 1979), 57.
7. Emil Gaverluk and Patrick Fisher, *Fiber Optics: Eye of the Antichrist* (Oklahoma City: Southwest Radio Church, 1979), 27.
8. Webber and Hutchings, *Apocalyptic Signs*, 33, 34.
9. Ibid., 34, 35.
10. Noah Hutchings, "God Makes the Headlines," *Gospel Truth* (September, 1982), 2.
11. Webber and Hutchings, *Apocalyptic Signs*, 54.
12. Ibid., 56.
13. Ibid., 53, 54.
14. Ibid., 1.
15. Ibid., 39, 40.
16. Ibid., 44.
17. Ibid., 44, 45
18. Hutchings, "God Makes the Headlines," 3.
19. Interview with Noah Hutchings on April 19, 1989.

20. William Alnor, "Long-time Southwest Radio Ministry Shaken by Financial Troubles," *Religious News Service* (December 9, 1988).
21. Noah Hutchings, *Marginal Mysteries* (Oklahoma City: Southwest Radio Church, 1986), 13.
22. Ibid., 29, 31.
23. Ibid., 27.
24. David Webber and Noah Hutchings, *Will Christ Come By 2001?* (Oklahoma City: Southwest Radio Church, 1978), 68.
25. Interview with David Webber on April 19, 1989.
26. Robert W. Faid, *Gorbachev! Has the Real Antichrist Come?* (Tulsa, Okla.: Victory House, 1988), 7.
27. William Alnor, "Conference for Cults Ministries Focuses on 'New Age' Issues," *Eternity* (May, 1985), 14 (*see* statement on the New Age movement).

Chapter 12

1. "Fulfilled Prophecy in Our Day," *God's News Behind the News* (January/February, 1988), 4.
2. Ibid., 5.
3. Mary S. Relfe, *When Your Money Fails . . . the "666 System" Is Here* (Montgomery, Ala.: Ministries, 1981), 119–126.
4. Ibid., 143.
5. *Current Events and Bible Prophecy Newsletter* (March–April, 1981), 5, 6.
6. "Book of the Year Awards," *Cornerstone* 13: 17.
7. Mary Stewart Relfe, *The New Money System* (Montgomery, Ala.: Ministries, 1982), "What they are saying" page.
8. Relfe, *Money Fails*, 17.
9. Doug Clark, *When Planets Align . . . (SYZTGY) EARTHQUAKE 1982!!* (Garden Grove, Calif.: Life Production Publication, 1976), 28.
10. Interview on the Southwest Radio Church broadcast, March 15, 1989.
11. Colin Deal, *Christ Returns by 1988: 101 Reasons Why* (Rutherford College, N.C.: Colin Deal, 1981), 120, 121.
12. Ibid., 150, 151.
13. Ibid., 50.
14. *Bible in the News* (July, 1979), 22.
15. David F. Webber and Noah Hutchings, *Will Christ Come by 2001?* (Oklahoma City: Southwest Radio Church, 1978), 54.

Chapter 13

1. Paul Goodman, *History of the Jews*, Israel Cohen, ed. (New York: E. P. Dutton and Co., 1959), 182.

2. Ibid.
3. M. E. Beirnes, "Occult Explosion: A Sign of the End," *Midnight Cry* (February, 1989), 7 (*see also* p. 15).
4. Ed Plowman, "The Legend(s) of John Todd," *Christianity Today* (February 2, 1979), 38.
5. Ibid., 38–41.
6. Ibid.
7. *Salem Kirban's Jerusalem Report*, no. 5, (1978), 1.
8. *Flashpoint—A Newsletter Ministry of Texe Marrs* (June/July, 1988), 1.
9. March 28, 1989 statement from Salem Kirban.

Chapter 14

1. Interview with Charles Taylor, April 20, 1989.
2. Ibid.
3. Ibid.
4. *Bible Prophecy News* 9, no. 7 (September, 1980), 2.
5. Charles R. Taylor, *Get All Excited—Jesus Is Coming Soon!* (Huntington Beach, Calif.: Today in Bible Prophecy, 1974), introduction.
6. Ibid., 93.
7. Ibid., 94.
8. Ibid., 89.
9. Charles R. Taylor, *Those Who Remain* (Huntington Beach, Calif.: Today in Bible Prophecy, 1980), 70.
10. Ibid., 71.
11. *Bible Prophecy News* 9, no. 7 (September, 1980), 2.
12. *Bible Prophecy News* 9, no. 8 (October, 1980), 2.
13. Charles R. Taylor, *Death of Sadat . . . Start of World War III* (Huntington Beach, Calif.: Today in Bible Prophecy, 1982), 85.
14. Charles R. Taylor, *Beware America—A Message to the President* (Huntington Beach, Calif.: Today in Bible Prophecy, 1983), 32.
15. Ibid., 42.
16. Charles R. Taylor, *When Jesus Comes* (Huntington Beach, Calif.: Today in Bible Prophecy, 1985), 17.
17. *Bible Prophecy News* 15, no. 1 (January, February, March, 1986), 6, 7.
18. *Bible Prophecy News* 15, no. 2 (April, May, June, 1986), 4, 6.
19. *Bible Prophecy News* 15, no. 3 (July, August, September, 1986), 2.
20. Ibid., 9.
21. *Bible Prophecy News* 16, no. 4 (October, November, December, 1987), 8.
22. Ibid., 11.
23. Charles R. Taylor, *WATCH 1988—The Year of Climax* (Huntington Beach, Calif.: Today in Bible Prophecy, 1988), 84.

24. *Bible Prophecy News* 17, no. 3 (July, August, September, 1988), 7.
25. Ibid., 5.
26. Taylor, *WATCH 1988*, 99.
27. *Bible Prophecy News* 17, no. 3 (July, August, September, 1988), 8.
28. Interview with Alexander Bobilev, Philadelphia, Penn., March 28, 1989.
29. Charles R. Taylor, *World War III and the Destiny of America* (Nashville, Tenn.: Thomas Nelson Publishers, 1979), 287.
30. Ibid., 367, 368.
31. Taylor, *Death of Sadat*, 91.
32. Ibid., 89.

Chapter 15

1. David Wilkerson, *The Vision* (Old Tappan, N. J.: Spire Books, 1974), 41.
2. Ibid., 27.
3. Ibid., 11.
4. Ibid., 29.
5. Ibid., preface. *Emphasis added.*
6. Ibid., 15.
7. Ibid., 16.
8. Ibid., 32.
9. Ibid., 34.
10. Ibid., 35.
11. Ibid., 27.
12. Ibid., 39.
13. Ibid., 51.
14. Ibid., 64.
15. Ibid., 82.
16. David Wilkerson, *Set the Trumpet by Thy Mouth—Hosea 8:1* (Lindale, Tex.: World Challenge, 1985), preface, 2.
17. Ibid., 2.
18. Ibid., 1.
19. Ibid., 14.
20. Frank Hammond, *In a Night Vision. God Warns America Arise, Oh, Church!* (Paducah, Ky.: David Alsobrook Ministries, 1985), 18.
21. Roxanne Brant, *My Vision: The Coming Calamities* (O'Brien, Fla.: Roxanne Brant Crusades, 1980), 31, 32.
22. Interview with James McKeever on April 20, 1989.

Chapter 16

1. Richard Woods, *The Occult Revolution* (New York: Seabury Press, 1973), 93.
2. John Ankerberg and John Weldon, *The Facts on Astrology* (Eugene, Ore.: Harvest House Publishers, 1988), 12.
3. Ibid.
4. David F. Webber and Noah Hutchings, *Apocalyptic Signs in the Heavens* (Oklahoma City: Southwest Radio Church, 1979), 28.
5. Colin Deal, *Christ Returns by 1988: 101 Reasons Why* (Rutherford College, N.C.: Colin Deal, 1981), 124.
6. Ibid.
7. William D. Banks, "Index of Star Names," *The Heavens Declare* (Kirkwood, Mo.: Impact Books, 1985), 247–258. Deal quotes the December 24, 1977, *Atlanta Journal* article as identifying the three stars as Sa as al Melik, Saad al Sund, and Scheat. Banks, a professing Christian, is a proponent of the "glory in the stars" theory. His exhaustive star-name index draws upon numerous works of others of like mind.
8. Webber and Hutchings, *Apocalyptic Signs*, 10.
9. Ibid.
10. Ibid.
11. Ibid., 9, 10.
12. Marcus Bach, *Major Religions of the World* (Nashville, Tenn.: Graded Press, 1959), 37.
13. Webber and Hutchings, *Apocalyptic Signs*, 10.
14. Ibid., 20.
15. Albert Dager, *The Gospel in the Zodiac* (Costa Mesa, Calif.: Media Spotlight, 1987), 6.
16. Banks, *Heavens Declare*, preface.
17. Dager, *Gospel in the Zodiac*, 8.
18. Ibid., 9.
19. Ibid., 66, 67.
20. Ibid., 11.
21. Ibid.
22. Ibid., 9.
23. Deal, *Christ Returns*, 123.
24. Ibid., 123, 124.
25. Webber and Hutchings, *Apocalyptic Signs*, 20.
26. Ibid., 24.
27. Ibid., 11.
28. Deal, *Christ Returns*, 123.

29. David F. Webber and Noah Hutchings, *Will Christ Come by 2001?* (Oklahoma City: Southwest Radio Church, 1978), 7.
30. "Prophets in the Last Days," *Gospel Truth* (November, 1981), 5.
31. Erika Cheetham, *The Prophecies of Nostradamus* (New York: G. P. Putnam's Sons, 1973), 5–12, 177.
32. Hall, *AD 1991—The Genesis of Holocaust* (Las Vegas, Nev.: Spirit of Prophecy Evangelical Ministries, 1985), 53.
33. Ankerberg and Weldon, *Facts on Astrology*, 22.
34. Ibid., 23.
35. Ibid., 22.

Chapter 17

1. J. R. Church, *Hidden Prophecies in the Psalms* (Oklahoma City: Prophecy Publications, 1986), 13, 14.
2. Ibid., 14.
3. Church, *Hidden Prophecies*, 16.
4. Ibid., 15.
5. Ibid., 246, 247.
6. Ibid., 248.
7. Ibid., 254–256.
8. Ibid., 260.
9. Ibid., 37.
10. Ibid., 149.
11. Ibid., 13.
12. Ibid., 150.
13. Ibid., 217.
14. Ibid., 72.
15. J. R. Church, "Prophetic Prospects for the Coming Year, 1989," *Prophecy in the News* (January, 1989), 5.
16. J. R. Church, *Why I Believe These Are the Last Days* (Oklahoma City, Okla.: Southwest Radio Church, 1989), 122.
17. Church, *Hidden Prophecies*, 244.
18. Ibid., 246, 247.
19. Dean C. Halverson, "88 Reasons What Went Wrong," *Christian Research Journal* (Fall, 1988), 18.
20. Edward C. Whisenant, *88 Reasons Why the Rapture Could Be in 1988* (Nashville, Tenn.: World Bible Society, 1988), 36.
21. John Warwick Montgomery, *Principalities and Powers* (Minneapolis, Minn.: Bethany House Publishers, 1973), 75.
22. Ibid., 80.
23. Ibid., 81.

24. Ibid., 80.
25. Church, *Hidden Prophecies*, 248, 249.
26. Montgomery, *Principalities*, 80.
27. Church, *Hidden Prophecies*, 260.
28. Montgomery, *Principalities*, 91, 92.
29. Oswald Allis, *Bible Numerics* (Chicago: Moody Press, 1944), 21.
30. Ibid., 22, 23.
31. Ibid., 24.

Chapter 18

1. *National and International Religion Report* (January 23, 1987).
2. "Signs of the Occult" paper, distributed by the Cult Awareness Network, Chicago, Ill.
3. Rick Branch, "LDS Predict the Second Coming!" *The Watchman Expositor*, no. 3 (1989), 4. (The book Branch was quoting from was by Francis M. Darter, who was not an official spokesman for the church.)
4. David Webber and Noah Hutchings, *New Light on the Great Pyramid* (Oklahoma City: Southwest Radio Church, 1985), 23.
5. David Webber, *A Satanic Trilogy: Pyramid Power* (Oklahoma City: Southwest Radio Church, 1979), 17.
6. Colin H. Deal, *The Day and Hour Jesus Will Return* (Rutherford College, N.C.: Colin Deal, 1981), 96, 97.
7. Interview with Doug Clark on April 11, 1989.
8. Reginald Dunlop, *Flee to the Mountains—God's Message for Survival—No Time to Spare—Imminent End-time Destruction* (Ontario, Calif.: Reginald Dunlop, circa 1975), 125.
9. Edgar C. Whisenant, *88 Reasons Why the Rapture Could Be in 1988* (Nashville, Tenn.: World Bible Society, 1988), 46, 47.
10. Ralph Lyman, *A Critique on the 1988 Rapture Theory* (Oklahoma City: Southwest Radio Church, 1988), 20–26.
11. Whisenant, *88 Reasons*, 46.
12. Edmond Gruss, *Cults and the Occult in the Age of Aquarius* (Grand Rapids, Mich.: Baker Books, 1974), 96.
13. Walter Martin, *The Kingdom of the Cults*, rev. ed. (Minneapolis, Minn.: Bethany Fellowship, 1965), 429.
14. Ibid., 428.
15. Wilbur Smith, *Egypt in Biblical Prophecy* (Boston: W. A. Wilde Co., 1957), 231.
16. Radford Neaum, *The Great Pyramid: A Prophetic Representation in Stone* (London: Simpkin, Marshall, 1930).

17. Smith, *Egypt*, 227.
18. Ibid.
19. Ibid., 221.
20. E. Raymond Capt, *The Great Pyramid Decoded* (Thousand Oaks, Calif.: Artisan Sales, 1971), 88.
21. Webber and Hutchings, *New Light*, 58.
22. Webber and Hutchings, *Prophecy in Stone* (Forth Worth, Tex.: Harvest Press, 1974), 65.
23. Colin Deal, *Christ Returns by 1988: 101 Reasons Why* (Rutherford College, N.C.: Colin Deal, 1981), 158.
24. Colin Deal, *Armageddon and the 21st Century* (Rutherford College, N.C.: Colin Deal, 1988), 81.
25. The sect, which was founded in 1918 by Paul Johnson, actively sells a 1,000-page book called *Great Pyramid Passages*, a forty-eight-page booklet called *The Great Pyramid and the Bible*, and *The Great Pyramid* tract. The Laymen's Home Missionary Movement headquarters is located in Chester Springs, Pennsylvania.
26. Capt, *The Great Pyramid*, 8.
27. Smith, *Egypt*, 217.
28. Ibid., 225.
29. Ibid., 227.
30. Ibid., 218.
31. Ibid., 224.
32. Philip Watson, *Egyptian Pyramids and Mastaba Tombs* (Buckinghamshire, Eng.: Shire Publications, 1987), 40.
33. Webber and Hutchings, *New Light*, 1.
34. Ibid., 42.
35. Smith, *Egypt*, 225.
36. Ibid., 229.
37. Ibid.
38. John Warwick Montgomery, *Principalities and Powers* (Minneapolis, Minn.: Bethany House Publishers, 1973), 53.

Chapter 19

1. William and Jacqueline Alnor's continuing series on Brother Stair and the "doomsday cult" began appearing on April 10, 1988, in the *Delaware County Daily Times*. Accounts of the stillbirth appeared in the July 8, 10 issues. *See also* page 6 in the Summer, 1988, and page 26 in the Fall, 1988, *Christian Research Journal*. Additionally, William was a 1988 guest on Fox Broadcasting's "A Current Affair" on the doomsday cults.

2. "The Mark of the Beast—666" *Overcomer* (March, 1988), 7.
3. To contact Mr. Lewis, write David A. Lewis Ministries, Inc., 304 E. Manchester, Springfield, MO 65810.

Chapter 20

1. *Prophetic Studies of the International Prophetic Conference* (Chicago: Fleming H. Revell, 1886), preface.
2. Interview with David Lewis on May 2, 1989.
3. David Lewis, *Prophecy Intelligence Digest* 6, no. 3, 3.
4. James J. Brookes, *Maranatha or the Lord Cometh* (St. Louis: Edward Bredell, 1878), 397, 412.
5. Dave Hunt, *Whatever Happened to Heaven?* (Eugene, Ore.: Harvest House Publishers, 1988), 269.
6. Garry Friesen, "A Return Visit," *Moody Monthly* (May, 1988), 30, 31.